Sir Alfred Mehran is an
has been trapped at Te
Gaulle Airport, Paris, for
sleeps, and lives his dai
from the airport's old 'B
the most famous homeles

THE TERMINAL MAN

SIR ALFRED MEHRAN
and
ANDREW DONKIN

CORGI BOOKS

THE TERMINAL MAN
A CORGI BOOK: 0 552 15274 9

First publication in Great Britain

PRINTING HISTORY
Corgi edition published 2004

1 3 5 7 9 10 8 6 4 2

Set in 11/14pt Palatino by
Falcon Oast Graphic Art Ltd.

Corgi Books are published by Transworld Publishers,
61–63 Uxbridge Road, London W5 5SA,
a division of The Random House Group Ltd,
in Australia by Random House Australia (Pty) Ltd,
20 Alfred Street, Milsons Point, Sydney, NSW 2061, Australia,
in New Zealand by Random House New Zealand Ltd,
18 Poland Road, Glenfield, Auckland 10, New Zealand
and in South Africa by Random House (Pty) Ltd,
Endulini, 5a Jubilee Road, Parktown 2193, South Africa.

Printed and bound in Great Britain by
Cox & Wyman Ltd, Reading, Berkshire.

Papers used by Transworld Publishers are natural, recyclable
products made from wood grown in sustainable forests. The
manufacturing processes conform to the environmental
regulations of the country of origin.

The authors extend their grateful thanks to the following people for their generous help in the preparation of this book: Christian Bourguet, Dr Philippe Bargain, Pasteur Jean-Pierre Dassonville, Carol Fontanille, Sophie Hicks and Matthew Rose. Thanks are also due to Stella Paskins, Claire Elliot, Glen Luchford, Jerry Stafford, Angela Troni, Annegret Scholz, Ellen Schoenfeld, Mike Fillis and Donald Trask. Thanks also to Vivien Francis – Human Rights Consultant. And special thanks to Barbara Laugwitz. May your documentation always be correct and your flight never be delayed.

Chapter 1

23rd May 2004

I am sitting on my red bench from the Bye Bye Bar in the middle of Charles de Gaulle airport, waiting to leave.

I am waiting for a green card so I can go to America. I am waiting for a British passport so I can go to England. I am waiting for my documentation so I can go anywhere.

I have been sitting on my red bench from the Bye Bye Bar in the middle of Charles de Gaulle airport waiting to leave for fifteen years.

Charles de Gaulle airport is 30km north of the city of Paris. My red bench is on the lower floor of Terminal One – a slab of 1960s concrete shaped like a doughnut ring.

Behind my red bench, a large glass window looks out onto the little open-air section at the very centre of the ring. It used to contain a fountain spouting water eighteen hours a day. The water kept getting dirty, so a few months ago the fountain was replaced by a garden planted with an uneasy mixture of palm trees and Christmas trees. I do not know if the garden will stay. I like the garden better because it makes less noise than the fountain so it is easier to get to sleep.

Above the new garden, escalators in silver walkways cut across the skyline, carrying passengers towards the planes that sit docked and waiting around the exterior of the terminal. You can get to anywhere in the world from here.

Passengers are reminded to keep their personal baggage with them at all times.

A tall woman with a mass of dark hair walks past my bench. I see her looking at me out of the corner of her eye. She is pulling a small suitcase on wheels and carries another bag slung over her shoulder.

I check my clock. It is 10:17 a.m. Around my bench are my possessions – my boxes, my bags, my newspapers. I reach behind my red bench and pick up a wad of A4 paper. On the top page I write: '23rd May 2004' and underline the date.

The tall woman walks past my bench again. She looks over, more obviously this time, hesitates, then pulls her suitcase and walks towards me.

'Excuse me, are you Sir Alfred?'

I tell her yes. She smiles.

'My name is Mandy Pink. Could I . . . could I talk to you for a few minutes?'

I tell her to sit down. In front of my red bench are a round black table and a chair, also from the Bye Bye Bar. When the bar closed down a few years ago, they gave me a special dispensation to keep the bench and the table and chair.

'I understand you've been here for quite a while?'

I nod. 'Fifteen years.'

'Fifteen years? And the whole time you've been . . .'

'Here.' I point to the red bench.

8

'Did you know you're quite famous?' asks the woman.

I say yes.

'I've just come from Australia. I work for a radio station in Tasmania and I've got a connection to London to catch in two hours.'

I ask her if it's hot in Australia.

She says sometimes.

'I read about you in a newspaper and I wondered if I could ask you a few questions? If you don't mind.'

I tell her I don't mind. I have many visitors. Many people asking questions. She takes out a radio microphone and puts it on the table. Also on the table is a plastic drinking cup; standing inside the cup are two McDonald's drinking straws in paper wrappers, three sachets of sugar, one sachet of salt, two sachets of pepper, one sachet of ketchup, two sets of plastic cutlery – a knife, fork, spoon, napkin – each sealed in a clear plastic wrapper.

'I'm really thirsty. Would you like a drink? A coffee or something?' she asks.

I say I would like an espresso and I tell her where the coffee bar is.

While she's gone I quickly take out my diary page for today and write down her name and what she has said to me. When I see her coming back, I stop writing.

'I didn't have any euros, but luckily they take English pounds.' She smiles and puts down my espresso, then she takes off her coat and leans forward to switch on her recorder.

'How did you come to be stuck here? In the airport?'

She puts the microphone under my nose and I tell her I am here because I do not have the correct documentation to leave. I cannot get on a plane because I do not have a passport, and I cannot leave the airport and go into France because I could be arrested by the French police for being an illegal immigrant and put in jail.

I tell her that in 1987 I was passing through Gard du Nord station, on my way to the airport to catch a flight to England. Gard du Nord is a big main-line station in north Paris, where people change from the metro to the overground lines that go out of the city. I was standing on the platform waiting for a train when I was mugged and my documents were stolen from my bag. I came to Charles de Gaulle anyway and caught my flight to London; in those days you could get on a plane without a passport, but you needed one at the other end. The authorities in London refused to allow me entry to the UK and I was returned straight back to Charles de Gaulle.

'And you've been here ever since?'

'Yes. Without my documents I could not prove who I was or where I should be.'

'How do you . . .'

Passengers are reminded to keep their personal baggage with them at all times.

The airport announcement system cuts over the voice of the woman. She grimaces.

'Does that repeat a lot?'

'Every ten minutes.'

'Even at night?'

'Even at night.'

'That must drive you a bit, you know, nuts?'

10

I nod.

'Sorry, I was asking you, how do you survive? How do you pay for your food?'

'In the beginning some members of the Lufthansa staff gave me food vouchers so I had a regular meal every day. Other companies as well, like Aer Lingus. They were very kind. Sometimes I earned some money by doing jobs for people in the airport, like translating when someone can't speak a language. Lately, I have money from television and film companies. So I can survive.'

'Where do you sleep?'

I point to the red bench. It's two and a half metres long and curved – designed to go round a large table in a bar.

'Is it comfortable?'

'Not really,' I say.

'How did you get to be called Sir Alfred?'

'Alfred was a nickname that I liked and then one day, many years ago, I had a letter from the British authorities which began with a mistake: "Dear Sir, Alfred . . ." I told a few people who thought it was funny and the name has kind of stuck since then.'

She asks how I spend my time. People always want to know how I spend my time. Whether it gets boring sitting in an airport for fifteen years on the same bench every day, looking across at the same shop window every day. I tell her it never gets boring. I have many things to do.

'Like what? What's an average day for you?'

'I wake up around 5:30 a.m. every morning. The sun comes in through the windows of the terminal. There are no curtains. I go to the men's washrooms early,

11

before there is anyone else there, so I can wash myself. There is no hot water so I have to wash myself every morning with cold. I have to be quick because I don't like to leave my possessions unattended. Anything could happen because I am not in a secure area.

'I spent the first eighteen months upstairs in the Departure hall. There was a Burger King up there with benches nearby – very comfortable. I only had one or two shoulder bags then, so I could move around fast. I could sit wherever I wanted in different bars, and different restaurants. I could move very quickly about the terminal, to anywhere I wanted, but over the years I have got more possessions, more bags, so that now it is not so easy.

'After I have washed, I usually get breakfast on my way back from the washroom. I used to buy a coffee and croissant, French breakfast, from Burger King, but they closed so now I have to get it from McDonald's. The airport starts to get really busy from about 8 a.m., with people coming down into the boutique level to buy newspapers or food.

'In the morning I might listen to the radio – maybe a French news station, to improve my French. Later I might write in my diary for an hour. I record who I see, what happens in the airport, my experiences, big news that I have read in newspapers. I have kept a diary every day since the middle of 1990. Dr Bargain from the Medical Centre gives me new paper whenever I finish a packet. There are four thousand sheets of past years' diaries in the Lufthansa storage boxes.'

I point to a pile of five grey boxes by the side of my bench.

'At lunchtime I have a Filet-o-fish from McDonald's and maybe an order of fries.'

'Do you have that every day?' says the woman.

'I must be their most loyal customer.'

She smiles.

'What else do you do?'

'In the afternoon, I read a book or a newspaper like the *Herald Tribune*, and maybe buy another coffee. Sometimes I have a visitor like you who wants to interview me. Sometimes I have a letter or official document that I have to reply to. I used to receive many letters. Whenever there was an article featuring me in a newspaper then I would get mail, from England, from America, from Canada, from people all over the world.'

'So you can receive letters here?' asks the woman.

'Not now. They used to keep my mail at the post office on this floor, and I would go along every few days and collect my letters. The postmaster was very helpful, but a few years ago in 1999 they stopped and now I can't receive mail any more.'

'So you don't get mail from your family? Or from friends?'

'I don't have any family. They are lost.'

12th April 1955

I am a child and there is water dripping down the back of my neck because Kaveh has just hit me with a damp cloth. Kaveh is my friend. He sits behind me in school and sometimes he makes me laugh in a lesson and we get into trouble from the teacher.

Kaveh laughs because now I have water running down the back of my neck.

I say, 'I will get you later.'

I am ten years old and my father has sent me to clean street signs because it is something useful to do. My name is Mehran Karimi Nasseri. I live in Masjed Soleiman with my family, where my father is a doctor for the company. The town of Masjed Soleiman is about 1,000km from Tehran in the west of Iran, quite near the border with Iraq.

I take my cloth from the bucket and as I raise my arm I send a spray of water towards Kaveh. He ducks. The sign we are cleaning says 'Naftak', which means 'little oil'. Most of the streets and areas are named after the oil wells. My father says that Masjed Soleiman is a 'company town', which means a whole town that is owned, designed and managed by a single company.

We finish cleaning the sign, pick up our buckets and walk towards the next one. Cleaning signs is a pointless job because everything always gets dirty again.

Masjed Soleiman only exists because of oil. In 1901, an Anglo-Australia prospector called William Knox Darcy bought the first oil concession in Iran. An oil concession is the right to look for and exploit oil in a certain area.

In April 1908, the first oilfield ever found in Iran was discovered at Masjed Soleiman. Darcy formed a company called the Anglo-Persian Oil Company, which later became the Anglo-Iranian Oil Company when our country changed its name to be better and more modern.

Before oil was found here, there was no Masjed Soleiman. The area was just barren mountains in a very deserted, mostly unpopulated area, where the only visitors were nomadic Bakhtiyari tribesmen who brought their herds of sheep to the hills to survive through the winter.

The first oil well that was discovered is called 'Nomre Yek', and sometimes when important people from the company come to Masjed Soleiman, they are driven to the well to look at it as if it is an important shrine.

After the oil was found, a refinery was quickly built, and then the town of Masjed Soleiman was planned and built around the wells and refineries so that workers could live close to their jobs.

Everything in Masjed Soleiman was built by the company: the houses, roads, schools, clubs, cinemas, and the hospital where my father works as a doctor. Being a doctor is a very respected job, although sometimes I think that my mother wishes he did not work there.

A few miles away is Abadan, another oil town also owned by the company. I have been there, when my father went to visit the hospital there. When you drive down from the hills, you can see from that distance that the streets of Abadan are in straight lines and everything is very neat. Masjed Soleiman is completely different because it is built in between hills and mountains, and has to fit around many natural features.

We are cleaning the next road sign which is for the neighbourhood of 'Camp Scotch' when I see Asghar running towards us.

'Come on. Quickly. They've got the bulldozer out!'

He turns and runs back the way he came. I drop my wet cloth and Kaveh and I run after him.

15

23rd May 2004

'You've been in lots of newspapers, but no-one from your past has ever contacted you?'

'No.'

'I read that originally you are from Iran, is that right?'

I tell her no, I'm not from Iran.

'Then where do you come from?'

I shrug my shoulders and she looks puzzled. I tell her that my point of origin has yet to be decided. I don't have any documentation.

'I was sure I'd read that it was Iran?'

I tell her no.

'So you've been living here at the airport for nearly *sixteen years*? What's the thing you miss the most? You know, about being trapped here. What do you really miss?'

'Marks & Spencer.'

'You mean the English chain store with clothes and food?'

I tell her that they had very nice things and that I miss walking down the shopping aisles and choosing what I would like to buy. There are not many shops in the terminal so I have little selection to choose from.

'Where do you wash your clothes? Is there a laundry here?'

I pick up a suit that is hanging on the back of the red bench. The suit is on a metal hanger and covered with plastic.

'There is a dry-cleaner opposite the restaurant area. I send my clothes there, and they wash and dry them for me and I collect them a week later.'

Would the last passengers for Flight 235 to Los Angeles please report to departure gate seven immediately.

'For free?'

'No, not for free.'

'Is there anything about Charles de Gaulle airport that you like?'

'Eventually, my departure.'

She smiles. Behind her I see a man loitering, watching us. He has a shoulder bag, and a large black camera with a silver flash is hanging round his neck.

'When do you think you might be able to leave the airport?'

I tell her I do not know. I have no passport. I cannot leave until I have the correct documentation.

'And where would you like to go when you do leave?'

I tell her that I'd like to go to maybe Florida or California.

The woman looks in her notebook to check that she has asked all her questions; then she checks her watch.

'Listen, thank you so much, you've been really helpful. I'd better get over to Terminal Two for my flight to London. When I get back to Tasmania in a couple of weeks I'll cut that tape into a radio interview.'

She stands up and we shake hands.

'Be seeing you.'

Behind her, the man with the camera is edging forward one step at a time, worried about intruding, but eager for her to leave.

She turns around to go and sees him. They exchange awkward smiles.

'Oh, are you waiting for . . .'

She says goodbye again and leaves, disappearing

around the corner with her suitcase on wheels following behind.

The man comes closer.

'Excuse me, are you Sir Alfred?'

I tell him yes. He smiles.

'My name is Donald Trask from Sentinel Radio. Could I . . . could I talk to you for a moment?'

I tell him to sit down. In front of my red bench are a round black table and a chair, also from the Bye Bye Bar. When the bar closed down a few years ago, they gave me a special dispensation to keep the bench and the table and chair.

'I understand,' says the man, 'you've been here for quite a while?'

I nod.

'Fifteen years.'

'Fifteen years? And the whole time you've been . . .'

'Here.'

'Did you know you're quite famous?' asks the man.

Diary extract
'8:05 a.m. I go to the washroom to shave and brush my teeth. Usually it is empty but today it is full because man says there is training course on third floor and their washroom is broken. I hope men will go soon. I like it quiet.'

Chapter 2

23rd May 2004

I am sitting on my red bench from the Bye Bye Bar in the middle of Charles de Gaulle airport, waiting for a man I don't know at all to start asking me questions.

His name is Donald Trask from Sentinel Radio in Philadelphia. He has a fat face, white shirt, blue jeans, and looks like a dentist.

'Do you mind if I tape this?'

Donald Trask takes a mini tape recorder from his bag and places it on the table. It is the kind that takes very small batteries. You cannot buy batteries of that size in the airport. You can only buy them in a shop through passport control.

People always want to know the same things.

Why do you stay in the airport? How did you get stuck here? How do you survive? How do you pay for your food? Where do you sleep? Is it comfortable? What's an average day for you? Do you really have a Filet-o-fish every day? What else do you do? What's the thing you miss most? When do you think you might be able to leave the airport?

Donald Trask from Sentinel Radio wants to know these things as well.

'And how did you get to be called Sir Alfred?'

I tell him the answer.

'When you were much younger, did you have any ambitions? Something that you wanted to do?'

'I have a degree in psychology. I used to think that I would like to have practice with patients coming,' I say.

'So you wanted to help people?'

'Yes.'

'You've been stuck in the airport for such a long time. Does that make you angry?'

I shake my head. 'Not angry. I just want to know my point of origin.'

'Could you tell me something about your childhood in Iran? Where did you grow up?'

I shake my head.

'No.'

'But you are from Iran?'

I shake my head again.

Passengers are reminded to keep their personal baggage with them at all times.

'No, my point of origin is not decided.'

Donald Trask looks confused.

'I am not Iranian. That was a false identity.'

Donald Trask looks more confused. He looks at his notebook, then gives up.

'Would you like a coffee?' he asks. 'I'm going to have one.'

I shrug my shoulders. 'Espresso.'

When he's gone I quickly take out my diary page for today, but I don't start writing because I have something else on my mind.

12th April 1955
'Quickly!'

Kaveh and I run with as much speed as we can. Cleaning street signs can wait. It does not take the bulldozer long to do its job and we will miss it if we are not quick.

Asghar, running in front of us, turns his head and shouts over his shoulder. 'They're in the wastes by Nomre-e Chehel.'

'Nomre-e Chehel' means Number 40 – the fortieth oil well to start producing.

We run around the back of the sports club and along the fence at the bottom of the swimming pool, because this way we do not have to go past the guard post standing sentry at the entrance to the only road to Nomre-e Chehel. Masjed Soleiman is set out so that different neighbourhoods are only connected with other parts of the town by narrow company-built roads. The land around the town and between neighbourhoods is just rough hillside.

Ahead of us we can see the crowd that has gathered. In the middle are grown-ups, with the children dancing around the edge of the group. I put my hand under my shirt. I run my finger along the scar on my stomach, where the knife cut me after people got angry when I told them what they should say.

21

All eyes are looking down into a small valley where the land falls away from the road. A land manager is halfway up the valley side directing a rusty and dirty bulldozer. The machine's tracks are sliding on the valley's muddy side and it is struggling to get a grip. The driver is pushing the gears into place – a movement that takes all his strength. Along the side of the valley slope is the bulldozer's target – a series of half a dozen ramshackle huts.

In Masjed Soleiman, the formal area of the town is laid out and planned by the company. Weaving between the formal areas are company roads, twisting and turning around the seven hills that make up the area. The formal areas have names that sound like England, such as 'Camp Scotch' and 'Western Hotel'. Outside the formal areas, places have local names like 'Sar Koureh' which means 'by the smokestack'.

Masjed Soleiman attracts many migrants looking for work. Sometimes people decide to stay in the hope of getting a job, or sometimes the company has a waiting list for houses. When this happens, the people build their own rough and ready homes. But the company does not like this because it undermines their control and so they order what is happening today. They order the bulldozer to go in and destroy the homes.

That is what we have come to watch.

23rd May 2004
'Alfred?'

I look up. Donald Trask is back at my table. The table is from the old Bye Bye Bar. They let me keep my red bench and my table because of special dispensation.

Donald Trask switches on his mini tape recorder again. It makes a faint whirring noise that you can only hear if you listen carefully and if there is no-one walking by with a trolley that squeaks loudly.

'Did you have any brothers or sisters when you were growing up in Iran?'

I shake my head.

'So you didn't have any brothers or sisters, right?'

The nail on the index finger of my left hand is longer than the rest of my fingernails; I rub it over my lower lip so that I can feel how smooth it is. I do this several times.

'Maybe. I don't know,' I tell him.

I pick up a newspaper and open it. It is a copy of *The Times* from yesterday.

I hold my newspaper up and start reading an article. Donald Trask sits in silence somewhere on the other side of the pages.

12th April 1955
In the beginning, the people built their homes on the flat ground, but the bulldozers always knocked them down easily. Now they build their huts in steep valleys, or by a cliff or a flood channel.

The man in the bulldozer grapples with the gear-stick to force it into reverse. The tread spins through the mud without getting a grip and the machine shudders but does not move. I do not think that it will be able to climb the side of the valley, so the houses will not be destroyed.

In a company town, a person's place and the kind of house they have depends on what job they do. There are many different clubs: one for senior staff and managers, one for junior staff, one for workers. My father is a doctor in the hospital, which is a good position to have, so we have a good house. In Masjed Soleiman everything depends on your rank. Workers and senior staff even have separate cemeteries for when they are dead.

The bulldozer strains against the side of the valley, but it is too steep. People watch and do not know whether they should cheer or be sorry. All of them work for the company and they must be careful. I hear a grating sound and around the corner of the hill comes another bulldozer. I recognize this one; its front is charred and burned. My father told me that they use it if there is a fire at one of the oil wells, to put the fire out.

The crowd watches as the bulldozer gets closer.

'This big one will get them,' says Asghar. His father also works in the hospital, but he is not a doctor, he is a cleaner.

The bulldozer leaves the road and heads up the valley side, passing the other stranded machine. Its thick tread bites into the steep slope and it slowly, slowly crawls up towards the huts that have appeared there. A woman in the crowd suddenly lets out a wail and holds her hands over her eyes.

Passengers are reminded to keep their personal baggage with them at all times.

The bulldozer touches the lowest hut and the entire structure collapses immediately. It smashes through what is left of the wall and careers through the other three structures as if they were made of paper. The remains of the shacks slide down the valley side; some pieces are so light that they nearly blow away in the

24

wind. In the crowd the woman is still wailing. This is usual.

The crowd starts to move off.

'Beat you to the bucket!'

Kaveh starts to run back to Camp Scotch. He looks behind, to make sure I am chasing him. I put my head down and run.

23rd May 2004

I turn over another page in my newspaper and begin to read an article about ex-President Clinton; it says that he is preparing a book about his life story. I am very interested in politics and if they have that book for sale in the newsagent's, I will buy it, although they only sell French-language version so I will need my French/English dictionary to assist me to read it.

'Alfred?'

I lower the newspaper and look at Donald Trask. He has turned off his mini tape recorder because no-one has been talking.

'Do you know that there is a film coming out that's based on your situation? A Steven Spielberg film?'

'Yes, of course. I signed the contract with Steven Spielberg–Dreamworks four years ago.'

'Not everyone gets to have Steven Spielberg make a film about their life.'

'No, of course not. Hollywood wanted to make a film about my situation because it is very unusual. It's not normal, living in an airport for fifteen years,' I tell him. 'It's a strange situation.'

'I've got an article about the film. Would you like to see it?'

I say, 'Yes,' but even if he shows me article about the Steven Spielberg film, I am not going to talk about being in Iran because I am not Iranian.

Donald Trask reaches into his black shoulder bag and takes out a copy of a magazine called *London Eye*. On the cover is a picture of the skyline of London with five coloured circles over it and the heading: 'The Olympics: Why We Need to Win'. Underneath in big letters it says, 'What Spielberg Did Next'.

Donald Trask opens the magazine to the correct page and gives it to me. This is what I read:

Adventures in Limbo
By Mike Fillis

Steven Spielberg's latest project is about Viktor Navorski, Balkan tourist, who becomes stranded at a major US airport when a political coup occurs in his homeland whilst he is flying to America, leaving him with an invalid passport and no means to return to his country.

Viktor must remain within the neutral territory of *The Terminal*, trapped until the great bureaucratic mechanism grinds sufficiently to determine his legal status and rescue him from the twilight zone of international limbo. Like Spielberg's other famous lost passenger, E.T., Viktor soon learns how to make friends and influence people.

Spielberg's first thought was to make the film on location. 'I originally wanted to shoot this at a real airport, but in the shadow of 9-11 it would be really impossible with all that security to bring in 125 crew members and 1,500 extras. It would have been a little impractical,' laughs the Oscar-winning director.

Instead, Spielberg found himself overseeing a huge construction project to build a full-size modern terminal akin to New York's John F. Kennedy – complete with four working escalators, fully staffed food outlets, and a host of product-placed retail outlets. 'It's the second largest set ever made for one of my films; the only set bigger was the one where the mothership landed in *Close Encounters of the Third Kind*!'

No expense was spared to replicate the modern aeronautical terminus of today, which was housed in 10,000 square meters of glass supported by 650 tonnes of steel and shrouded in a white Ultrabounce cloth to suggest the glare of daylight. Real luggage conveyors and working departure displays were installed along with a gamut of fully stocked food outlets that kept the myriads of 'passengers' fed. Only the skyborne airliners were added digitally in postproduction.

If Spielberg seems to have swapped illegal aliens from space for illegal aliens from the Balkans, it's perhaps because he was inspired by the extraordinary real-life odyssey of Mehran Karimi Nasseri, better known as Sir Alfred, and his sixteen-year layover at Charles de Gaulle airport just outside Paris. Trapped there without the documentation that he needs to leave the airport or catch a flight, Sir Alfred has lived for sixteen years (since August 1988) on the same red bench. He has eaten a McDonald's Filet-o-fish for lunch every single day of his long wait.

Sir Alfred's story first reached Hollywood in 1995, but being an idea rather than a story it took a while for it to be shaped into a working screenplay, let alone one which would attract the very cream of Hollywood talent like Spielberg and Hanks.

The story's co-creator Andrew Niccol (*The Truman Show*) explains that the similarity ends there and that it took months of careful craftsmanship by the film's writers, Sacha Gervasi and Jeff Nathanson, to take Sir Alfred's situation and turn it into a story. Tom Hanks's character certainly has an eventful time as he falls in love with a Nebraskan flight attendant played by Catherine Zeta-Jones and becomes entangled in the copious red tape of US customs official Frank Dixon (Stanley Tucci). Dixon is the 'villain' of the piece since he considers Viktor to be a potential security risk, but he must also accord the refugee all the rights of a democratic society.

Nevertheless, Steven Spielberg said that 'because Sir Alfred is the only other person, to our knowledge, living quasi-permanently at a major international airport, we thought it would be prudent to buy the rights to his story.' The deal, rumored to be around $300,000 and a cut of the box office, is generous by any standards and has ironically given the stranded Iranian the financial freedom to do as he pleases.

The tag line for the film's poster is 'Life is Waiting' – for Viktor the implication is that it's waiting outside the Terminal if he can only defeat the bad guy and get out to it. As far as the real Sir Alfred is concerned though, for him the actual process of waiting is life and has been for sixteen years.

Tom Hanks is no stranger to the lonely leading role, having played a lost desert islander in *Cast Away*. There he was truly alone, devoid of food, water, shelter, and, above all, company. *The Terminal* brings a loneliness of another kind – one of isolation in an antiseptic, self-sustaining microworld that promises excitement and adventure further afield, the loneliness felt amongst indifferent crowds deeply intent on being elsewhere. It is the loneliness of the itinerant, of the homeless whom people do not wish to see.

In this serious comedy – as producers Walter Parkes and Laurie MacDonald are wont to describe it – Viktor is shown in detail living his daily routine, eating, washing, surviving, and touching the lives of those fleeting travelers who cross his path.

Hanks always seems able to mine that vein of likeability from the depths of the eccentric characters he portrays. Spielberg says of his star: 'He entertains me. Sometimes I just sit by the monitor and stifle the laughter so that it doesn't ruin the take he's doing. I just love his improvisational skills.'

Of particular joy to Hanks, and a prime cause of Viktor's communication problems with the rest of the airport, is his accent and phraseology. Hanks studied this in detail with a dialect coach and claims he struggled with a largely Bulgarian accent – making every effort, he says, not to end up sounding like Dracula. The end result in the movie is both convincing and frequently very funny.

It's a peculiarity of this particular production that the many, many hours actors would normally have to idle away, waiting for camera to be set up and lighting to be rigged, were spent browsing through the real bookshops and duty free shops that had been built on set to provide the verisimilitude of Viktor's world. At one point, Catherine Zeta-Jones was spotted in the newsagent's, hiding a magazine with her on the cover so that it wouldn't appear in shot in the next scene.

Hanks describes it as 'the antithesis of working on most movie sets which are usually hot and dusty' and riddled with cables. The whole experience of making *The Terminal* was actually more like waiting for your connecting flight at a real airport. 'You have a few phone calls you can make, you sit back, you wander around and you actually kind of enjoy it.' Unless, of course, you're the real Sir Alfred, in which case it might be some considerable time before that connecting flight actually arrives.

I turn over the page and there is a picture of a man I don't know smiling, and a heading that says: 'Ron Fogelman, British Producer tells us – "Why Brits are Hits in Hollywood".' This is another film article but not on Spielberg.

'What do you think of it?' asks Donald Trask.

'I don't have Filet-o-fish every day for sixteen years,' I tell him. 'That's wrong. I have only eaten it since they opened, maybe nine years.'

Diary extract
'8:15 p.m. Workers in the CD shop arrived early this morning and began to put Christmas decorations in the window. Looks pretty. I hope they do not have flashing lights like last year. Look nice, but very hard to sleep with flashing lights at night.'

Chapter 3

23rd May 2004
Donald Trask from Sentinel Radio in Philadelphia is still asking me questions. He still has a fat face, white shirt, blue jeans, and he still looks like a dentist.

Donald Trask switches on his mini tape recorder again. It makes a faint whirring noise that you can only hear if you listen carefully and if there is no-one walking by with a trolley that squeaks loudly.

'I just need a few details of your background in Iran for my story. For example what kind of house did you live in?'

I wave my finger.

'I cannot talk about that. I never agreed to be interviewed about that. I will only talk from time of leaving the country. I can only talk about after I left Iran because I am not Iranian,' I tell him.

'OK, Alfred,' says Donald. 'Tell me what happened *after* you left Iran. Tell me everything.'

This is what happened after I left Iran.

19th September 1973
In the last week my life has changed completely. I have flown from Tehran to Heathrow airport, London, which was the first time I have been on aeroplane, then I took the train to Bradford. I have come to England for a three-year university course.

I am standing under a bus shelter in the middle of Bradford and I am running out of time. I have to get to the university building and produce my documentation so that I can register for my course. Today registration closes at 4:00 p.m., so I must show my documents before that time to be accepted.

A bus comes; I check the piece of paper in my hand, which has on it the number of the bus that I require. The landlord of the house where I am staying wrote the number there. The landlord told me that he has never had a tenant from Iran before. I told him I have never had a landlord from England before, and he laughed. This morning he had dried yellow fluid on the front of his shirt. I believe it may have been fried egg. He does not keep himself nice.

I get on the bus because the number on the bus matches exactly the number that the landlord with the dirty shirt wrote on the paper for me.

I was going to ask the bus driver to tell me when we reach the university, in case I do not recognize it, which was also a suggestion of the landlord. But I do not think such a request will be necessary because there are many students on bus. I will watch them and get off at the same location.

After making eight stops that are not the university, the bus makes a stop that is the university. I recognize this for two reasons: first, all the students get off the bus and walk towards the university; and second, because there is a big sign which says 'Bradford University'.

As I get near the steps of the building I see a hand-written sign that says ENROLMENT MAIN HALL. I walk up the steps and inside, and follow the directions.

The main hall is full of people in lines. I choose the shortest line and wait. I check my documentation, which is all present and ready.

'Hello. Are you doing Physics too, then?' says a man with red hair and a sports bag. On the side of his sports bag is the word ADIDAS. Someone has written words after each letter in a blue biro pen so that it also reads: 'All Day I Dream About Sex'. I do not know if this is true because you cannot tell such a thing from looking at someone's sports bag.

'No, I am not doing Physics,' I say.

'Chemistry?'

'No.' He looks at me with expectation. I say, 'I am doing Yugoslav Studies.'

'You're in the wrong line then, mate. This is for the Science faculty.'

So I change lines. But I do not choose the next shortest line because that does not necessarily signify Yugoslav Studies. Instead I look at what is written on the sign on each desk. I cannot see a sign that says 'Yugoslav Studies', but I can see a sign for the faculty that includes Yugoslav Studies so I walk there and stand in that line.

After a few moments, the man who has come to stand behind me says, 'Hello.'

I have to turn around. I do not really want to turn around because then I will not see when the person in front of me moves forward, and I might lose my place because the queue keeps moving. So I have to stand awkwardly, half facing the person in front of me, and half facing the person behind. And I have to watch both of them. This is not easy.

The person behind me wears glasses with thick, black rims, and a round face that is shaped like a flat, white plate. He is smiling and has a blue and white scarf wrapped around his neck.

'Hello, I'm David. David Headley,' he says, putting out his hand.

'I am Mehran Karimi Nasseri.' I shake his hand.

He tells me what course he is doing. Not the same one as me, but also history of Europe. 'And what are you doing?'

'Yugoslav Studies. It is a three-year degree course.'

'Have you ever been to Yugoslavia?'

'No. But I would like to go one day.'

'Did you study Yugoslavia in Iran?'

'No, my degree there was in Psychology, at the University of Tehran.'

'What is Yugoslav Studies then?'

'The brochure says it is making study of Yugoslavia history, language, culture, economy. Many things.'

'And you just fancied it?'

'Yes,' I say. 'I had to leave Iran by special arrangement and I saw an advert in *The Economist* magazine and began correspondence with the university. I was accepted by letter and I receive money from Iran to attend.'

The woman in front of me has moved away from the table and now it is my turn.

'I have to go now. Please excuse me,' I say to David Headley.

'Next!' says the lady sitting at the table.

I explain to the lady the reason why I am here in Bradford University is to study Yugoslav Studies.

'And do you have your documents?' she asks.

I reach into my pocket and pull out all the documents I need.

10th October 1973

Sometimes when I dream I remember opening my eyes and seeing doctors moving around me, talking in a strange language. There's a white sheet over part of my body.

I was at home in my family house in Tehran. I wanted to turn on the television so I leant round behind it to plug it into the socket on the wall. As my hand touched the socket, there was a flash of blue electricity. My other hand was touching the television set. I felt electricity spark out from that hand and into the metal of the television set. Then I don't remember anything until I woke up in hospital with doctors over me, looking down. I can still feel the electric shock in my hand.

Sometimes in this memory the people standing over me do not look like doctors at all.

2nd March 1974

There are people all around me. The air is warm and full of sweat. I do not like it. I have to be careful not to trip up the man in front of me, or become trampled by the person walking behind me. David Headley has his arm looped in my arm. I do not really like that either, but it is a good protection against falling down. It would not be pleasant to fall down.

We come to a straight section of road and the march moves forward in an unsteady surge, as if it were a giant creature that has swallowed me. I am helpless inside it and can only wait to see what will happen.

I think of how I got here. I think of this morning. I woke at 6.00 a.m. and I did not need my alarm clock. Something in my head can tell what time it is when I am sleeping, if I have to get up at a particular moment.

Today is not a normal day of attending a lecture, or spending time studying in the library. I enjoy reading magazines and newspapers to improve my English language. When I awoke today I washed and dressed quickly and went straight to Bradford railway station because that was where we were meeting.

When I arrived, I was the only person of my group to be there, but soon other students from the university appeared. Many of them were yawning. They did not put their hand over their mouth when they yawned even when they were speaking to someone.

Many people brought banners that they have made. The banners have slogans on them saying bad things about the Shah and expressing their wish that he should leave power soon.

'Hello Mehran,' says a voice behind me.

I turn and see that it is Martha Johansson. She

stretches up on tiptoe and kisses my cheek. She is an American and we are on the same course. She is very intelligent and has no problem with her Yugoslav translation. She does not need to spend as much time in the library as I do.

David Headley is the organizer, but he was almost last to arrive. He wears glasses with thick black rims, and has a round face that is always smiling. He usually wears a blue and white scarf wrapped around his neck. One day last term he got very upset because someone said that he looked like Rupert the Bear. I do not know Rupert the Bear. Martha Johansson told me this was not a good thing to say about David because Rupert the Bear is a character for children. He lives in a place called Nutwood and his best friend is a badger, which is an underground animal that only exists at night and has a black and white coat.

David told everybody to go onto the platform to wait for the train. A few men in suits gave us strange looks and a few smile at the girls. At 7:31 a.m., we caught the 7:23 a.m. train which was running eight minutes late, and we travelled to London.

Passengers are reminded to keep their personal baggage with them at all times.

The train terminated its journey at Kings Cross, a great, dirty station that smelled of oil and petrol. At Kings Cross we went down an escalator and caught an underground train to our destination.

David checks his watch. 'Ten to eleven, at least we missed rush hour.'

He is from London. His parents are quite rich, I think, and he supports Chelsea Football Club.

When we arrived at Charing Cross on the Northern

Line, there was a queue to get out of the station because there were so many people going to the same place.

'We'll be all right as long as the rain holds off,' Dave tells us.

When we were finally out of the station and in the open air, the people raised their banners and signs and we joined the protest march against the Shah.

The Shah has kept power in Iran by ruling with terror. Many thousands of people were tortured and executed; most of them were political prisoners who disagreed with the Shah. People could not speak or write freely in newspapers; all dissent was suppressed.

In Iran itself, the universities had become the centres of the political opposition to the regime of the Shah. They were joined by student opposition in other countries, organized by the Confederacy of Iranian Students – a group that was formed in Germany. Most Iranian students came from a background of the middle classes or even better-off families, because it cost a lot of money to study abroad and poor families could not afford it.

In the summer of 1967, the Shah made an official visit to Germany because he wanted to promote more business between the two countries. When he arrived, thousands of students came to protest in front of the German opera house in Berlin. One student, Benno Ohnesorg, was killed by a policeman and it became a very famous case.

The idea of having protest marches was to draw attention in Britain, Germany, France and America, to events that were occurring in Iran under the Shah. The

Confederacy of Iranian Students wanted to see three things: democracy, social justice and the return of Ayatollah Khomeini who had been exiled by the Shah. I do not think either will be possible while the Shah is living there.

How this Shah came to be in power in Iran explains much of the reason why many Iranians resent the West, and America in particular. To understand the origin of this Shah, it is necessary to look back to when the First World War was being fought in Europe, when much of Persia, as the country was known then, was occupied by Britain and Russia. The British were in the south and the Russians controlled much of the north. The Shah at that time was Shah Ahmad. The British thought that this Shah was growing weak and were worried about what might happen next – both because of the Russian occupation in the north, and also because Germany was occupying neighbouring Iraq.

So the British decided to support an army officer called Reza Khan and helped him organize a coup d'état. Reza Khan set up a puppet prime minister to be in control of the country. A few years later, when things seemed to be going well, he proclaimed himself prime minister instead. He decided that the country needed to be modernized in many ways. There was little transport available in the country, there were hardly any hospitals or doctors, there was little industry except for oil, and few people in the normal population could read and write.

He also decided that the country needed a new, modern name and so he changed it from Persia to Iran. The word Iran came from the word 'Aryan', which means 'from noble birth'.

There was much trouble in Iran during the Second World War. The newly named Iran stayed neutral in the war between the Allies and Germany, but Britain and Russia (once more controlling many parts of the country) were worried that Reza Khan might decide to support Germany. He was forced into exile in South Africa and he died three years later.

His 22-year-old son, Mohammed Reza, whose thinking was always very pro-West, took Reza Khan's place as ruler of Iran. He is the Shah that is still in control today.

He nearly lost power in the early Fifties and he had to flee the country, but the American CIA planned a coup to get him back into power because they wanted access to Iran's oil. They got their way and the Shah returned to rule over Iran and its people.

The Shah instigated some changes that became known as the White Revolution. Some things he did were good, like making sure more people were taught to read and write, and making other things more modern. But many things were not popular with the *ulema* – the religious powers.

One example of something very bad was that the Shah approved a law bill which meant that American soldiers in Iran could not be arrested or prosecuted, no matter what they did. This particular bill was opposed very strongly by Ayatollah Khomeini, who said in quite a famous quote that the Shah had 'reduced the Iranian people to a level lower than an American dog'. He said this because if a person ran over a dog in America, that person would be arrested, but if an American ran over an Iranian in Iran, he would go free. Ayatollah Khomeini was soon exiled by the Shah because of his criticisms.

The Shah is now married to his third wife, Farah Diba, the daughter of an army officer. He divorced his first two wives because neither of them gave him a male heir. Only a male heir is eligible to succeed to the throne, so he divorced them in the hope that a third wife will produce one.

To keep himself in power, the Shah relied more and more on silencing and killing his opponents. Protests against the Shah and his regime have been growing every year. The Shah makes much money from selling oil to America and the West, but the money does not go to the people because the Shah spends it on building new palaces and on buying weapons from arms merchants. Most normal people find their conditions getting worse as inflation makes what little money they have worth even less.

People are not free to protest in Iran, even at the universities, without the risk of being arrested and put in jail to be tortured or killed. So other people, like student activists, must protest against the Shah's regimen in countries like England, where it can be done without danger. That is why I am here today, because I do not have to worry about being arrested for marching against such things.

It is now quarter past four in the afternoon. It has been raining since lunchtime. The sky is grey and it is getting darker. We have marched from a long road called The Strand outside Charing Cross station, through Trafalgar Square, along Pall Mall and past Buckingham Palace where the Queen of England lives. Perhaps she was watching from a window, but I do not know. I did not see her.

41

As we go through the gates into Hyde Park, there is a line of press photographers standing on a raised platform, taking photos.

'Front page,' says David with a smile. 'Be everywhere tomorrow.' He gives me the thumbs up sign, which means that he thinks things are good.

We trail inside the park, onto a grass field that has been turned into mud by many feet. There is a small stage at the front of the crowd where a politician that I do not recognize is speaking through a microphone. I cannot hear what he is saying.

My feet hurt and there is water inside my shoes. Still, I would rather have rain than too much heat and dust.

Diary extract

'11:35 a.m. I leave my bench and walk to the post office to collect my mail. There is a copy of *Time* magazine received on my subscription and also a letter postmarked: Helsinki, the capital of Finland. Inside is a piece of paper that says 'I READ ABOUT YOU IN A NEWSPAPER. LET ME GIVE YOU THESE LOVELY ROSES' and an old postcard with a picture of some roses lying on a table. The red of the roses is very dark and rich. On the back of the card is a postmark that says 1920 and five lines of Finnish writing in black ink. It is beautiful and I lean it against the plastic cup containing two McDonald drinking straws that is on my table.'

Chapter 4

7th August 1975

Two men in uniform are standing over me, watching me carefully. One of them has a long black stick; the other one has a gun. I am in trouble.

I am sitting on the ground in a completely empty room. The floor is dusty and cracked and in the middle of it is a dark stain. It is very hot and I have not had any water to drink for a long time. I do not know exactly how long because I do not have my watch or any of my possessions.

I landed at Tehran airport many hours ago. I queued with my passport and waited for the police to check me.

'Where are you coming from?'

'London.'

'What were you doing in England?'

'I was a student for two years.'

The policemen exchanged looks and told me to wait for a moment while they checked some information. Then I was brought here to Evin prison on the hillside in Tehran. It is a prison built by the Shah and run by the most hated organization in the entire country, the Savak, the Iranian secret police.

I remember my father telling me why they were created. When the Prime Minister, Dr Mohammad Mosaddeq, nationalized the oilfields in 1951, the West boycotted Iranian oil in revenge, which led to great economical problems. Two years later, the Shah was forced to leave the country and flee and Dr Mosaddeq became leader. The West was not happy and combining with ambitious elements in the government, the American CIA organized a political coup that returned the Shah to power.

Having gone to all that trouble to get the Shah back on his throne, America did not want to lose him again, so in 1956 the CIA helped and guided the Shah in the creation of the Savak. This organization was created for one reason and one reason only – to keep the Shah in power.

They had two reasons. First, because America wished to protect their interests in Iran's massive oilfields, and second, because they saw the Shah as a useful obstacle preventing the expansion of the Soviet Union to the north of Iran. Many people in Iran came to hate America because of this act.

Savak is an acronym for Sazmann-e Amniyat va Ittilait-e Keshvar, which translates as the Agency for Security and Information. It is the Savak's job to protect the Shah's regime and eliminate any threats to its continuation. Soon after it was formed, the Savak became a law unto itself with the power to arrest and imprison anyone it liked without specific charge. Over the years, the Savak has executed and tortured thousands of people for political reasons.

Savak activities also include gathering intelligence on enemies or potential enemies of the Shah. The Savak has its own censorship office to watch and control writers, students and academics in universities. They have bought special electronic devices from American companies that allow the Savak to listen in on telephone calls made anywhere in Iran. The Savak does not have to justify its actions to anybody.

If an Iranian speaks to someone from a foreign country about politics, then he will always speak to that person individually – never within a group. This is because he knows that another Iranian might be secret informer for the Savak.

Interrogation and torture methods in Savak prisons include, but are not limited to: electric shocks, whippings, beatings, inserting broken glass into a person's body, the forced extraction of teeth, the forced extraction of fingernails, the forced extraction of toenails, tying weights to the testicles, and pouring boiling water into the rectum.

I remember this information because it was in a newspaper in the library at university and I copied out the paragraph into my page-a-day Letts diary and Martha Johansson saw me writing it and asked me what I was doing and why didn't I just cut out the article from the newspaper although the newspaper was not mine to cut up. I do not have the list now because the list is in my diary, and my diary is in my luggage and my luggage has been taken by the Savak.

I am sitting on a dusty floor and I am thirsty and hungry. I avoid looking at the two guards standing in the room just across from me. I do not wish them to see me looking at them. They are bored and are talking quietly. I do not wish to remind them that I am here.

The nail on the index finger of my left hand is longer than the rest of my fingernails; I rub it over my lower lip so that I can feel how smooth it is. I do this several times.

There are sounds outside in the corridor and the two men watching me look towards the metal door of the room. It opens and in walks a Savak officer with papers under his arm. Two more men follow behind him; they are carrying a small wooden table and two chairs.

The two men set out the table and chairs and then leave. The officer sits on one chair, puts his files on the table, then points to me and then to the other empty chair.

I struggle to get up. My leg is stiff from sitting on

the floor. I sit opposite the officer; I do not ⬛
table. The two men in uniform, who have been wa⬛
ing me for an hour, stand behind me in the shadows
in the corner.

'Do you know why you are here?' asks the officer.

'No.'

'Are you an opponent of the Shah?'

'No.'

'Have you ever acted to oppose the regime of the
Shah?'

'No.'

'Have you ever marched in protest against the
Shah?'

'No.'

I ask for a drink of water.

'Why have you returned to Iran?'

26th April 1975
Four months earlier.
I am standing under a bus shelter in the middle of
Bradford and I am running out of money. It is raining.
I like the rain. It is better to have too much rain than
too little rain and sun all the time. I put my hand in
my pocket and bring out some bronze coins.

I am running out of money quickly. Every three
months I should receive money in my bank account
from Iran. I have had nothing since before the
month of November. I have several letters from
the university saying that they have not received the
money for my tuition. I am a foreign student and they
require money to teach me and allow me to attend my
Yugoslav Studies course. I have a special arrangement
that I should come to England and study at an English

...y university fees, lodgings and
...d be paid for.

...e correct number on the front pulls
...nd I pay my fare.

...e money did not arrive in November, the
...g I did was wait to see if it would arrive in
...ber, but it did not arrive in December. I wrote a
le..er and waited, but I did not receive any reply. After that I tried phoning, but the telephone line made a strange noise which people told me means that the number does not exist.

I can continue to wait, to see if any money comes into my account soon, but if I leave it for much longer I will not have enough money left to be able to buy a ticket to fly to Tehran to discover for myself why the money has stopped arriving.

I get off the bus and walk into the university building. I am early and I know people from my course will be waiting in the cafeteria.

Sitting at one table is David Headley, and opposite him is Martha Johansson.

'Hello, Mehran. Have you done the essay?' says Martha.

'Yes.'

'Will you show me,' she asks with a wide smile. She always says this, because she knows that I cannot show her my essay because it would not be the correct procedure to show someone else my work.

'No.'

Everyone laughs.

'Are you still waiting for a letter?'

I tell her yes.

'There's an airmail letter in your pigeon-hole. I saw it when I checked mine.'

I have time to get the letter before the lecture starts. The fifth time I wrote, I used the university as my address because I suspected that the landlord where I rent my room may be hiding my mail and stealing it for reasons which are not clear or known to me. However, neither David Headley nor Martha Johansson agree with this proposition.

I get to my pigeon-hole and take out the letter. It is a light blue airmail envelope that I posted myself approximately one month ago. On the front, in Farsi, is a black ink stamp that says: 'Unknown – Return to Originator'.

7th August 1975

I am explaining myself to an officer of the Savak. I am explaining why I have returned to Iran and what I am doing here, in the hope that he will not order people to pour boiling water into my rectum. The nail on the index finger of my left hand is longer than the rest of my fingernails; I rub it over my lower lip so that I can feel how smooth it is.

'I was studying in England, but I had to return because I received no word and no money for six months,' I tell him.

'Why?'

'I do not know. I have tried to get in touch: writing letters, making phone calls, sending a telegram. The telephone is not answered and the letters are returned unopened. The only thing left to do was buy a plane ticket and come. I had to discover why the money for my university has stopped.'

'You were arrested at the airport?'

'First they made me wait and then, yes, I was arrested.'

'Why do you think you were arrested?'

'I don't know.'

I ask him again if I can have a drink. He asks the two uniformed guards how long I have been in here and one of them says, 'Four hours.'

The officer says, 'Good.' Then he picks up the file from the table and looks through it at the same time as watching me. Then he asks me exactly the same questions that he has already asked me.

'Do you know why you are here?'

'No.'

'Are you an opponent of the Shah?'

'No.'

'Have you ever acted to oppose the regime of the Shah?'

'No.'

'Have you ever marched in protest against the Shah?'

'No.'

Then he takes out a photograph from the file and puts it on the table facing me. It is a picture of a crowd of people. In the middle of the photograph someone has circled my face with a thick black marker pen. Next to me is a man wearing glasses with thick black rims. He has a round face and he is smiling. Around his neck is wrapped a blue and white scarf.

'Go and make sure they are ready for us downstairs,' says the officer to one of the guards. He leaves the room.

The officer looks at the photograph and taps it with the first finger on his right hand.

'Now do you know why you are here?'

13th September 1975

Sometimes when I dream I remember opening my eyes and seeing doctors moving around me, talking in a strange language. There's a white sheet over part of my body.

I was in my house in Tehran. I wanted to turn on the television so I leant round behind it to plug it into the socket on the wall. As my hand touched the socket, there was a flash of blue electricity. My other hand was touching the television set. I felt electricity spark out from that hand and into the metal of the television set. Then I don't remember anything until I woke up in hospital with doctors over me, looking down. I can still feel the electric shock in my hand.

Sometimes in this memory the people standing over me do not look like doctors at all. They have different uniforms and the electric shock is getting worse. I feel it in my hand and my arm. But I do not like to think of this.

14th December 1975

I cannot tell how much time has gone by in this dark place under the ground. I think I have been here for probably three months. In the first month, they used to take me out and ask me questions. Sometimes there was electricity. But I think they have decided that I do not know anything.

Every afternoon, the guard delivers half a bowl of food. It is not pleasant but I am always hungry.

The cell next door to mine is empty again. The person inside swore and struggled when they came to take him out. Guards put him on the floor and kicked him until he did not move again.

It is cold at night now, but there is no blanket in the cell. There is no bed to put it on.

From the passageway outside I hear the footsteps of the guard bringing my food bowl. He is early today and his footsteps are lighter. Maybe it is a different guard. Instead of sliding the bowl through the metal hatch, he stops and unlocks the door. I feel a knot tighten in my stomach.

As the door opens, I see that it is not the guard, but an officer. He turns his nose up at the smell inside the cell.

'Stand up.'

I stand up. My left hand trembles slightly when I lean upon it. I remember the accident with the television and electricity.

'You're leaving,' the officer tells me.

'Leaving?'

'Someone from your family has paid money to fix your situation and you are leaving.'

'Someone is here?'

'No, of course not.'

I cannot tell him. No-one outside the family knows the truth. Everyone here still thinks that my family is my family. It is a great shame on a family's name to have the son of a doctor in prison. They are rich and they have paid money to get me out. This is common practice.

I follow him down the corridor. I walk slowly because I have been in one place for a long time and my leg is sore.

'You will be taken to the airport and put on an

aeroplane. You will be given an immigration passport, which is valid for just one year. You are forbidden to return to Iran.'

'Where will aeroplane take me?'

'I don't know,' says the officer. 'That is not my problem.'

Diary extract

'7:35 p.m. A woman with a trolley rushes to the shop doorway but the shop is shut and it is locked up. She swears loudly. She looks around and then she pushes her luggage trolley over towards me. Her trolley is stacked with many things. She looks at my belongings that surround my red bench.

"I need to buy a case because they won't let me on the plane with all this hand luggage. Could I buy one of your cases?"

"No, I need it," I tell her.

"I can give you fifty dollars."

I shake my head.

"But the shop is shut and you've got lots."

"They are full."

She takes hold of one of my Lufthansa boxes and tries to move it. She sees that it is very heavy.

"Sixty."

I tell her that I cannot sell my Lufthansa boxes and that she should ask the airline for her own.

She swears directly at my person in unpleasant manner and leaves.'

Chapter 5

16th November 1977

Outside the train it is snowing, and inside the windows are running with condensation. I am cold and my jacket is wet.

The aeroplane from Tehran took me to the United Kingdom where I applied for entry. I was refused so I appealed. I was refused again. My strong proposition is that I should be in United Kingdom. Firstly so I can finish my course and secondly because I wish to for personal reasons which I cannot speak of.

But I have not been accepted by the United Kingdom so I have spent the last two years moving around and waiting for responses from authorities. Now I am going to West Berlin to apply for asylum in West Germany.

Sitting opposite me on the train are two Australian tourists. One is called Bill and one is called Mary. Bill has small bright eyes that look straight at you. It has been a long journey and I know many things about them. They are married. They are retired. They have been visiting Bill's brother in London. Mary likes to walk around old churches in the countryside. Bill likes to write poetry.

'And do you know what we got in here, mate?' He taps the side of the Nikon camera that never leaves his hand.

I tell him that I do not know what is in his camera.

'Only the bloody Queen of England,' he says, his eyes becoming very large. 'We were waiting to cross the road to go to Hyde Park and this big black car stops at the traffic lights, and who's bloody sitting in the back, mate, if it's not the bloody Queen. So I says to my missis, "Gotta get a snap of that." So I just snap her sitting in the back of her car. Wait till they see that at home. It's the bloody Queen. Last thing we took in London. Film's still in here.'

Outside the snow is easing and we can see white trees go rushing by the side of the train. Bill aims his camera but there is nothing to photograph except a blur of snow crystals on branches.

'So where are you going, then?'

'West Berlin.'

The train does not go anywhere else.

'You having a bit of a tour like us?'

I am going to West Germany because I requested asylum in United Kingdom but they refused me, so I appealed but they refused me again, and then I requested asylum in France but they refused me and so I appealed but they refused me again, and then I requested asylum in Netherlands, but they refused me so I appealed but they refused me again.

'Yes,' I say, 'I am having a bit of a tour.'

Bill smiles. 'Great.'

The train begins to slow down, creaking and bumping as it loses speed. I hear the sound of straining metal. Bill looks out of the window searching for something. 'Is this it? Is this the border? Wait till I tell my son, Russ, that we've been through the Iron Curtain. Like James bloody Bond.'

After the Second World War, the city of Berlin was divided into four zones: the British, French, American and the Russian. But the entire city itself was in the Russian section of Germany that became East Germany. So the three zones that the Allies controlled are like an island of the West in East Germany. In 1961 the Russians built a wall around West Berlin to make sure that the citizens stayed in East Germany and could not escape to the West. In the 1970s, transit routes were opened to allow people from inside the city of West Berlin to travel to West Germany by car or by train. The transit routes go through East Germany and no-one is allowed to leave the specific routes as they make the journey.

The train has stopped at Griebnitzsee. This is the border between west and east. The station platform is short and we are in the rear carriage of the train so it looks as if we have stopped in the middle of nowhere.

'Look at that.'

To either side of the station there are high fences with watchtowers scattered along them. Behind those fences is the *Todesstreifen* – death line.

Click.

The snowfall has reduced to a few flakes and Bill starts taking photographs of the watchtowers through the window. I do not think this is a good idea.

Outside a soldier in a dark green uniform with a large Alsatian dog walks slowly along the side of the train. The soldier looks dispirited, and whenever the dog slows down he pulls it along in sharp jerks. The dog is old and tired.

The door from the next carriage opens and in come two border guards. Each has a pistol tucked into his belt. They must check the documentation of everyone on the train. I do not know what they will say when they see my passport.

One border guard has a large stomach and a chubby face; the other has a moustache like Stalin. The one with the moustache has a sort of vendor's tray that he uses to lay passports on when he has to stamp them.

I do not see either of them smile at anyone. They go through the carriage checking every person's papers while people sit quietly, not saying anything. German passengers must be used to this.

Click.

Bill takes a photograph out of the window, of the guard with the Alsatian dog. Inside the carriage, the guards' eyes move in the direction of the camera noise. Mary sees this. Bill does not.

'Stop taking photos. I don't think they like it,' she tells her husband.

The border guards glance at West German passports and take their time over all other papers. They are not really interested in passports; they want to be sure that there are no East Germans on the train escaping into West Berlin. That is the main reason they are here.

Bill takes another photograph out of the window. The guards stop looking at passports and move in our direction. They reach the seats next to us.

'Good day,' says Bill.

Bill raises his camera and takes a photograph of the border guard with the large stomach and chubby face.

'You don't mind, do you? We're from Australia. We're having a bit of a tour and . . .'

The guard with the large stomach and chubby face snatches Bill's camera from his hands, presses a button and flicks open the back of the camera. With his other hand, he rips out the film so that it spirals out of the back. The film is exposed and will not operate correctly now.

'Jesus H. Christ! The bloody Queen!'

The border guard with the large stomach and chubby face hands the camera back to Bill without saying a word.

The guard takes Bill and Mary's passports from Mary and he and the other guard examine the documents, slowly turning over every single page. The rest of the carriage sits in silence. Even Bill.

Finally they hand the passports back to Mary and, without even looking at me, they continue through to the next carriage.

When they have closed the doors behind them, Bill holds up the ruined film. Bill's wife shakes her head in a way that says, 'I told you to put it away. Now look what has happened, and it is all your own fault.'

So Bill holds out the twisted, tattered, useless film to show me.

'Dingo's bollocks, mate. That was the bloody Queen.'

After a few minutes the train begins to move forward again, heading into the city of West Berlin. The first station is Bahnhof Wannsee, where a few German people depart from the train.

'You know anywhere good to stay?' asks Bill.

I say, 'No.'

I have never been to West Berlin before. Bill and Mary start to take their luggage down from the overhead racks as the train slowly creeps into Bahnhof Zoologischer Garten. Everyone rushes for the doors.

'Well, so long, mate,' says Bill.

The station is not more than six platforms, which is not very big considering that it is the main train station for West Berlin. The platform I am standing on is raised high above the ground and around it are glass walls so that I can see out to the streets around the station. This is the famous glass hall.

I leave the station by the main entrance and as I step out onto the pavement my foot skids across the snow and I nearly fall. Many footsteps have turned the light snow into sheets of ice. I walk carefully. I cross a big square with many cars parked in rows and many yellow double-decker buses heading in different directions.

Then I hear a noise like a very powerful trumpet. I am standing in West Berlin, it is snowing, there is ice under my feet, and I can hear elephants. Across the street I see a large picture of a giraffe and a sign that says 'Zoo'. I wonder if the animals know that this place of ice and snow and cold is not where they belong.

I sit in a bus shelter and open my bag. Inside is a piece of paper with the address of a youth hostel given to me in Brussels by a man who said he had stayed there. I find a newspaper shop that also sells street maps, and I open a fold-out map of the city to look for the address.

I do not understand what the man behind the counter is saying, but I think he does not like me looking at the map without first buying it. But I have seen the street name and memorized my route to the correct location, so I can return the map to the shelf. I have a problem because the map is very hard to fold away. I try to follow the way the map is creased and fold it away in the same direction, but it does not work. I try folding it down in a different way, but this does not work either. I try again.

The man behind the counter stops serving a customer and comes over to me. Quickly, he takes the map from my hands. Then he grabs the collar of my jacket and throws me from the shop. He is a very rough man and I do not like him.

When my feet touch the ice on the pavement outside, I slide and cannot stand up properly because the man has pushed me out. I fall over onto the ice and impact on my right hip and my right elbow. I drop my bag. A woman holding the hand of a small child helps me up and says something nice in German, but I do not know what.

I remember the location of the youth hostel – in a back street not far from the big shopping area of the Ku'damn. It is dark now and people are leaving their jobs to go home. I find the address, but the youth hostel is no longer there. Instead, in its place is a carpet warehouse. The window is full of Persian carpets. Most of them are Toyserkan designs from western Iran. One carpet displayed at the back is from Qom and displays an image of hunters on horseback chasing goats. Very nice.

There is a small sign on the door that says where the nearest youth hostel is located, but it sounds very far away so I find a café that is still open and buy a cup of coffee to try and warm myself up. Then I walk back to the station. I do not have enough money for a hotel, which would be very expensive. I decide that I should try and find somewhere to spend the night inside the station, and then in the morning I will look for the youth hostel.

I walk round to the back of the station, but I cannot see any suitable place to stop. There are no cafés open where I could sit, or even a bar. There are several women standing on the edge of the pavement, just waiting there. They are dressed as if they are going to a party.

Just inside the station three homeless people are sitting wrapped up in blankets, leaning against the wall. One of them has a plastic cup on the floor and next to it is a little sign that he has written in German. I do not know what it says because I cannot read German, but I do not think it matters because it is not addressed specifically to me.

A boy, maybe fourteen or fifteen years old, has been watching me and now I have noticed him he comes towards me. He is wearing a dirty anorak, and under the anorak he is wearing a jumper but no shirt. I can tell this because the jumper has some holes in it and I can see his bare skin under the jumper. His hair is greasy and lies flat on his head.

He stops in front of me and looks at me as if he thinks I might say something, but I have nothing to say because I do not know him. Then he speaks quietly in German. I shrug my shoulders, so then he makes gesture with his hands and mouth, like a sucking gesture, and when I see this I understand that he is offering to give sex for money. I walk away very quickly because it is very embarrassing to say such a thing, and I do not think he should say it to me. It is very bad.

I sit on a bench near the entrance to the station. It is a public area but it is empty, not like the back of the station where there are many people offering you things that you do not want to buy.

There are two people at the place where you change

money. Now they have finished and turned around I see that they are Bill and Mary.

'Good day, mate.'

They have changed their clothes so I did not recognize them from behind. Mary has a scarf over her head.

'We found a nice little hotel around the corner from the bloody zoo. I had to come back to change some more money to take the missis out for dinner. I've got to keep her sweet, haven't I?'

Bill looks at me and then around at the empty station.

'You all right there?'

'I am waiting for some friends to come and meet me.'

'Your mates were supposed to meet you from the train and they didn't turn up?'

I nod.

'They will come soon,' I say.

Mary leans into Bill and whispers something. I cannot hear what she says. Bill looks surprised by what he has heard. He thinks for a moment, then reaches into his pocket, brings out a black leather wallet and takes out a banknote.

'Here, mate. I changed a bit too much money just then. Can you use this for me.'

I shake my head.

'Please, mate, it's not a problem.'

'But you will need money to buy a new film for your camera,' I say.

'New film?' Bill laughs. 'Listen, I've got loads of bloody films, all right? It's not a problem.'

He hands me the money and I take it.

'Look after yourself, OK?'

Mary puts her arm through his and they walk off. They are very nice people. I now probably have enough money to find a cheap hotel, but I should not need to take money from people and I feel ashamed because that is what I have done.

I will apply for asylum in Germany. If they do not accept me I will move on and try a different country.

I leave the station, but I do not go through the back way because there are many people there who offer you things that you do not want to buy and I do not like it.

Diary extract
'Nothing changes for me except I have more baggage. Other passengers stay in the airport for a few hours. They arrive on plane and go to cars or buses or trains that are waiting for them. Or they arrive and travel through electric tube to departure gate. I am here ten years. When it's my turn, when I am called, I am ready to go.'

Chapter 6

22nd January 1981
I am sitting in a library in Brussels reading a newspaper, waiting for the result of my request for asylum in Belgium. I will not know the result for many months.

I applied for asylum in Berlin, West Germany, four years ago. They refused. Since then I have applied in the Netherlands – refused; I appealed – refused. In '78 I tried France, but France would not permit me entry and my request for asylum was refused. I appealed. Refused. After France I tried Yugoslavia where I believe I had good chance of entry because I can speak the Yugoslav language and I could make a good case for why they should admit me. Yugoslavia refused me. In '79 I tried Italy. They refused me.

In 1980 I tried France again, but they refused me once more. I appealed against the first refusal, but they didn't allow my appeal, so I had to appeal again. They refused. I requested to emigrate to the United Kingdom, but they refused again. I flew to Heathrow airport, London, but they would not let me enter and in August 1980 they expelled me.

I tried to travel to West Germany once more to request asylum there, but when I reached Hamburg I was arrested by German police and escorted to the frontier with Belgium. Belgium let me enter because the German police said that was where I had originated from.

On 23rd October 1980, I requested to be classed as a refugee by the United Nations High Commission for Refugees in Brussels. UNHCR was established in 1950 by the UN General Assembly so that it could protect refugees and resolve refugee problems. Now I must wait months for the result of my application.

This morning I am sitting in a library for two reasons. First, because it is cold and the library is heated better than the youth hostel where I am staying. Second, because I wish to read a newspaper and they have free newspapers in the library. I wish to read a newspaper because yesterday a bit of history was made. The hostage crisis between Iran and America is over.

On 4th November 1979, a group of about 400 Revolutionary Guards stormed the American Embassy in Tehran and seized control, taking the Americans inside hostage.

The embassy was seized partly because the exiled Shah had been admitted to the United States of

America for medical treatment and Iranian militants did not like this idea. The other reason was to demonstrate the strength of the new Iranian regime and how it did not fear the USA.

The Iranian Prime Minister, Mehdi Bazargan, tried to solve the situation and had to resign. Very soon, Ayatollah Khomeini gave the militants his blessing anyway, describing the American government as the 'Great Satan'.

As the embassy was stormed, there was much confusion and six Americans escaped into the nearby Canadian Embassy. The Canadians gave them fake Canadian passports and with this forged documentation they were able to leave without being noticed as Americans.

The seizure of the embassy had many serious consequences. President Jimmy Carter stopped oil exports from Iran, expelled some Iranians from the USA, and froze $8 billion worth of Iranian assets that were in the USA.

A few months after the embassy was seized, Iran issued a set of demands for releasing the hostages. These included the return of the ex-Shah to Iran, and an apology for past American interference in Iran which had kept the Shah and his Savak secret police in power. They also wanted a promise that America would not interfere again in the future. A team of negotiators went to Panama in South America, but their talks did not bring a breakthrough.

America decided not to wait for the hostages to be released and attempted a rescue mission in April 1980. It was called Operation Eagle Claw, but it ended badly. Some American helicopters secretly flew into the Great Salt Desert of south-eastern Iran, but three out of eight of the helicopters were badly damaged in a sandstorm. When they tried to take off again, catastrophe struck as one helicopter hit a transport plane and crashed, killing eight soldiers.

The entire occurrence was bad for the American President, Jimmy Carter, who lost the election to Ronald Reagan.

Last year two important things happened which made the Iranians want to end the situation. The first was that the Shah died while in Egypt. The second was that Iraq had begun to invade western Iran and it looked like a long war might be starting. The Iranians wanted the hostage situation over so that they could concentrate on other things like fighting the war.

Yesterday, 21st January 1981, Ronald Reagan was inaugurated as America's new president and the USA released the $8 billion of Iranian money they had frozen; finally the hostages were released and flown to Germany. The 52 Americans had been held captive for a total of 444 days. Very bad for them.

7th October 1981

For the last year, I have spent most of my days sitting in the public library in Brussels studying. This morning I have come to UNHCR because they said I had to come on today's date to collect the result of my request for refugee status.

While I wait for my appointment, I ask the man behind the counter for a form so I can appeal their refusal when I receive it. He takes out a blue form and stamps the top with a date stamp which says 7th October 1981 – today's date.

Then someone calls my name. I enter the interview room, which is where you have to go when your proceedings are private and other people cannot hear your conversation. My appointment is with a man who is wearing a little silver badge of Tintin on the lapel of his blue jacket.

He asks me to sign a document, so I sign it and then he hands it to me and puts out his hand.

I ask him why.

He says, 'Mr Mehran, you are now accepted as refugee.'

On the front of the document that he gave me it says: *'Nations Unies Haut Commissariat pour les Réfugiés – Délégation en Belgique Certificat de Réfugié'*.

Inside there is a small picture of me, which I had attached to my application form when I completed it last year. It is not a bad picture, but I am leaning to one side and there is some shadow.

Inside it says: 'From the convention regarding the status of refugees agreed upon in Geneva on 28th July 1951 passed into law on 26th June 1953. The holder of the present document, Karimi Nasseri Mehran, is acknowledged as a refugee in the sense of the Geneva Convention. Brussels, 7th October 1981.'

I am accepted.

'Is there anything else?' the man says.

I am accepted.

'If you go out through the door . . .'

Finally I am accepted.

The man shows me the way out of the room, although the way out is obvious because there is only one door.

71

As I walk out onto the street, I remember what is in my bag so I go back inside.

'Thank you but I do not require this,' I say to the man behind the counter.

I hand him back the form for making an appeal against refusal.

I do not need it.

3rd March 1984

I am sitting in the room that I rent in the youth hostel. The room is paid for by social services in Brussels. I am looking at a notebook in which I sometimes write notes like a diary. I am reading back what I have just written so that I can remember it well. This is what I have just written.

Diary extract

'I was reading in the library today when I was interrupted by a man.

He asked me my name and said, "Yes, I have heard of you. You study in here every day."

I said, "Yes, most days. Not on Sundays because library is closed on Sundays, and not on Saturday afternoon after 4:30 p.m. because library is closed on Saturday afternoon after 4:30 p.m."

The man said, "The librarian told me your story: that you travelled round Europe and you were rejected by every country for years and years until finally you were accepted by Belgium as a refugee."

I said, "Yes."

The man said, "I used to work in Iran. I used to travel around supplying equipment for their medical facilities for the Anglo-Iranian Oil Company. It was my job to keep them stocked with everything from bandages to operating trolleys."

I said, "My father worked for them; he was a doctor in a hospital."

Then we spoke about very personal things that I will not write in this diary, because in the daytime when I am in the library, someone could take this diary from my room and read it and discover things that are not their concern. So I will not write them here.

Then the man said, "Do you know the name of that British nurse?"

I said, "No, I was never told and I cannot ask now."

The man said, "What town was it? Masjed Soleiman, yes?" Then he thought for a few seconds and said, "Miss Semon. Yes, that would have been Miss Semon."

I said, "Do you know her?"

The man said, "I do not know her myself, but the last I heard she was living in Glasgow in Scotland."

I could not think of anything to say to the man, so I did not say anything. Then the man said, "It was nice to meet you. Good luck if you decide to try and find her."

Then he walked off towards the modern history section, which is in the front section of the library under the big glass windows near the door.'

End of diary extract.

I read this in my diary once more, and then once again. I cannot remember anything about the man except that he was wearing a dark suit and his shoulders were wide, but his head was narrow like a pencil. I do not think this can be correct.

10th July 1984

My proposition has changed. My proposition is no longer that I live in Belgium and study to improve my English in the library. My proposition is that I should go to the United Kingdom, so I am standing in a queue in the British Consulate so that I can get a stamp on my documents to allow me to enter the United Kingdom.

I cannot get a passport from the Iranian authorities because I am not Iranian. I must receive a document called *Titre de voyage*, which is not the same as a visa but which fulfils the same function. To get this, I had to show my refugee card at the prefecture and fill in a form with many questions and many boxes.

17th April 1986

I am standing on the bow of a ferry sailing out into the North Sea. I am forty-one years old and the sun is shining on my face. The boat is rocking with the waves that hit the stern.

I am going to England to find my origin. I have been through passport control leaving Belgium and I am now on an English ferry heading for England where I will become a British citizen. In my hand is an envelope. It is not sealed.

Passengers are reminded to keep their personal baggage with them at all times.

Through the North Sea mist I see an oil tanker slowly creeping into view, becoming larger and larger on the horizon like a building sailing through the water. At least, I think I remember the oil tanker. I am not sure when I saw the oil tanker, and when I remember things again this time there is no tanker.

I go downstairs into the bar and buy an espresso. I take it outside to where I can see the sea and sit at a table. I open my shoulder bag and take out my refugee card and my permit, stamped by the British Consulate, which allows me permission to visit England.

At last they will not refuse my proposition to enter.

Diary extract

'3:15 p.m. Man from airport authorities comes down to the boutique level and goes into every shop giving out a piece of paper. The paper says: "*SUITE AUX EVENEMENTS SURVENUS AUX ETATS UNIS, AREOPORTS DE PARIS ET LES COMPAGNIES AERIENNES S ASSOCIENT AU GOVERNMENT FRANCIS ET VOUS PRIENT DE BEIN VOULOIR RESPECTER 3mn DE SILENCE ET DE RECUEILLE-MENT A 12H00 VENDREDI 14 SEPTEMBRE 2001 A LA MEMORIES DES VICTIMS DE CES CATASTROPHES.*"

He gives me a copy because he says "you are part of airport too." '

Chapter 7

8th August 1988
It is two years since I left Belgium and always the authorities still refuse to let me enter the United Kingdom. I have tried to enter by flying and also by travelling by boat. Always they refuse me. This morning I came to Terminal One, Charles de Gaulle airport, and flew to Heathrow airport, London, but immigration officials would not let me into Britain. They said that I did not have the correct documentation. I

explained the reason I was coming to England, but still they would not let me enter.

They made me wait while the other passengers from the plane went through passport control and then they took me to a room away from the public area and asked me why I was trying to enter the country illegally. I waited in the room and a man brought me a very bad cup of coffee.

After another hour, they took me outside and put me on a flight back to Charles de Gaulle airport. When we landed I had to wait in my seat on the plane until the other passengers had gone. Then French immigration officials came on board and escorted me off the aircraft. They took me through passport control and brought me to the public area of Terminal One.

I do not have anywhere else to go so I walk around the terminal and sit down on an empty bench.

Sitting on the bench next to mine is a man who has a very thick beard, with a rucksack next to him on the floor. He is holding an American passport and is looking through it. Even from here I can see it has many stamps from different countries inside.

'You got many stamps in yours?' The man has seen me looking at him.

'Sorry. I was not looking.'

'It's all right. Airport blues – nothing else to do but flick through the pages of your own passport. You know? While you wait.'

I nod.

'I'm on my way home to Chicago. Which one's yours? Cairo?' says the man, pointing to the departures board, which shows the numbers and times of all the departing flights.

'No. I have already flown to the United Kingdom, but they sent me back to Charles de Gaulle.'

'No, really? Why didn't they let you in?'

Passengers are reminded to keep their personal baggage with them at all times.

I tell him that I do not have the correct documentation. I do not have a British passport. I do not have any passport. I do not have any documentation.

'What happened to your passport?'

'I had a travel permit and refugee papers from the Belgium authorities. But now they are gone,' I say.

'They expired?'

'No, stolen.'

'When?'

'Last year. A thief took them at Gare du Nord. Mugging.'

'Man, that's terrible. What happened?'

I tell him the following events occurred.

7th August 1987

I am at Gare du Nord standing on the RER platform waiting for the B3 train to Charles de Gaulle airport. I am wearing light trousers, a short-sleeved shirt, and I am carrying a shoulder bag that contains everything I own in the world.

The streets are full of sweating tourists. Deep under Gare du Nord, the tunnels feel like an oven. An overweight woman sits down on the plastic seats and mops her forehead. A section of platform recently repaired with black pitch oozes under my feet.

'Excusez-moi. Pouvez-vous m'aider?'

A man is speaking to me. He is tall and thin and unshaven. I open my mouth to tell him that I do not speak French, when I feel another man grab the strap of my bag. He rips it from my shoulder with both hands. The first man that spoke to me pushes me in the chest and knocks me off balance, so I fall back onto the platform. I turn my head and see the man with the bag running along the platform towards an exit staircase. The man who pushed me is running after him. They are thieves working together. They have taken everything.

I pick myself up. The fat woman shakes her head in sympathy. I run after them, down the first staircase. I nearly trip. At the bottom of the stairs, the tunnel breaks into three forks leading to other platforms and other lines. You can get to anywhere in Paris from here. People pass through Gare du Nord. No-one stays.

I take the left tunnel, but there is no sign of the men. My arm hurts where I fell. I catch my breath. My shirt is suddenly cold and wet on my back. They have taken everything.

After an hour of searching, I see my bag sticking out of a litter bin three levels up, on the D platform for trains heading north to Orry-la-Ville. Inside is a paperback book, but everything else has vanished. Although they will be no use to the thieves, they have taken my documentation. My refugee papers are gone.

The top of my bag is smeared with a mouldy banana skin from the bin. The banana skin is mashed into the metal teeth of the zipper. I start to wipe it off, but it just makes more mess.

(None of this really happened.)

8th August 1988

4:54 p.m. The American man looks very concerned. 'Did you call the cops?'

'No, what can they do?' I shrug my shoulders.

'So what will you do now? You going to go to your embassy or something?'

'No point. They cannot help. I want to get to England, but I must wait here until I can get a ticket.'

Flight 23AD to Chicago is now boarding from gate five.

'That's me. I better go, or I'm gonna get stuck here too.' The man is embarrassed at the awkward joke. 'Look, do you need some bucks for coffee or something?' he says, putting his hand in his pocket.

'Thank you. I have money,' I say. This is not true.

'Take care, OK? It was really cool meeting you. You're a well-travelled dude. You'll find a way to get to England.'

I am a well-travelled dude.

The American picks up his backpack and leaves. He gives a wave as he reaches the electric tube that takes passengers up to the boarding gates, then he is gone. No-one stays long in an airport.

8th August 1988

7:40 p.m. It is evening and the airport is getting quieter. Planes are leaving, but no new passengers are arriving. The man in the Burger King keeps looking at his watch every few minutes, waiting for his shift to end at 8.00 p.m. when they close. He clears the wrappers and rubbish that customers have left on the tables and then wipes the tables with a damp cloth. I am the only customer left. I will buy another black coffee before they close.

Passengers for flight VJF70 to Rome are requested to make their way to gate 23 immediately. We apologize for the earlier delay.

I am stuck at Charles de Gaulle airport. Since I have lost my documents I cannot move. If I leave the airport I have no papers so I can be arrested as illegal immigrant and be sent to prison. If I fly on a plane I cannot pass passport control and I am returned to Charles de Gaulle airport. I want to get a plane to England, but without correct documents, England always refuses me.

I walk to the counter of Burger King. The staff are in the back cleaning the machines and cooking devices. When one of them sees me waiting, he shakes his head.

'*Fermé.*'

The last planeload of passengers has left the terminal to board their aircraft, heading to their holidays or their homes. Cleaners are sweeping the floor. I take a walk down the stairs to the boutique level in the basement. The shops have metal shutters over their windows and doors. There is a bar called the Bye Bye Bar that is closing as well.

The terminal is shaped like a large ring and I walk right around the basement level in a circuit to see what is down there, and then I come back up the stairs.

Outside, the sky is getting dark. Just near Burger King are the long benches where I was sitting this morning, waiting for my plane to England. I go over and sit down. I put my shoulder bag with some clothes in it at one end, and then lie on my side along the bench using my bag as a pillow. It is not a usual proposition to sleep in an airport, but it is only for one night.

9th August 1988
I wake up early in the morning because I am sleeping by the windows, so when it gets light it awakens me immediately. Burger King opens at 7.00 a.m. and I buy a French breakfast. I take a walk downstairs to the newsagent, to look at the newspapers. Many newspapers are reporting the ending of the Iran–Iraq War and I buy a copy of the *International News Herald*.

In 1980, Saddam Hussein, the President of Iraq, thought that Iran was in some confusion after the downfall of the Shah. He decided the time was right to invade the Khuzestan province, so that he could steal the area's oil. Saddam Hussein sent troops and Iraq military across the border into Iran, to invade and to claim this territory. Of course, there was a war.

Although the Iraq military was much better equipped, the Iranians stopped arguing with each other and joined forces against the enemy. By the summer of 1982, Iran had forced the Iraq military back to their border, but then the Iranian generals wanted to push the fighting into Iraq to capture two towns, Najak and Karbala, because both are important sites of pilgrimage for Shiite Muslims. The fighting near the border resembled the trench warfare of the First World War, with many dying from poison-gas attacks.

Finally today, they have arranged a ceasefire, and after eight years of fighting the war is over. The article says that half a million people on each side were killed. During the Iran–Iraq War, the West was on the

83

side of Saddam Hussein because they trust him more than they trust Iran.

I read the newspaper story from start to finish. Eight years after the war started, and after one million deaths, the borders between the two countries are exactly the same as when they started.

When I finish the article, I take a walk around the terminal. It is shaped like a ring, so soon I am back where I started.

Diary extract
'4:15 p.m. I was listening to the news on the radio and when I switched it off I heard the man and woman on the bench next to mine speaking Yugoslavian. I remembered language. I heard dialogue about their baby that the woman is holding. They were drinking beer and the baby had a small doll. I was very excited to hear the Yugoslavian language because I have not spoken in such a language since I left university many years ago. I decided that I would show them a book that I have on the subject of Yugoslavia and engage them in conversation as an opportunity to practise my spoken Yugoslavian. I took my set of keys from my pocket and found the correct key and unlocked the small padlock on the bag and then I sort through the contents but I could not find the book. I found an interesting article about President Clinton and I read that instead. My proposition was that it might contain information about Yugoslavia, but it did not. When I looked up to speak to Yugoslavian man and woman they had gone. Baby also.'

Chapter 8

4th November 1988

I have been living in Terminal One, Charles de Gaulle airport for three months. In the night I sleep on a red bench near Burger King. In the daytime I walk around the terminal. I only have one shoulder bag with me so it is easy to move around. If I leave Terminal One then I am worried that outside I will be arrested. People know me here so I am not likely to be arrested. When I tried to buy ticket I receive conversation with them. Workers for airline gave me vouchers for food which I can take to Burger King or other restaurant and exchange for French fries. I want to get to United Kingdom so I will remain in the airport until I have enough for a new ticket which looks now like a good possibility.

Last week, the passport control here in the airport had a problem with a family who arrived. The family only spoke Farsi. Farsi or Persian is the language spoken in Iran and no-one at the airport speaks it. So one of the people in passport control who knows me, came and asked me if I would go into the special security area to act as a translator for the airport. I said that I did not speak Farsi but that I would act as translator. It was a very important job for me, for one or two hours.

I told the passport officer that, in a book, Farsi is written as Arabic script and it is read from right to left. He said that this fact was totally irrelevant to the situation.

The people who needed a translator were a father, mother and their two daughters, aged eight and ten.

They had arrived on a flight coming from Rome, with no documentation and they wanted to make a claim for asylum in France.

'*Salam aleykom,*' I said, which means 'hello'.

They were all quite scared, and the woman was almost frantic.

'*Na mifahman. Na mifahman! Lotfan un o benevisin.*'

I explained to the passport-control officer that the man was saying that he could not understand him. And could the passport-control officer please write down what he was saying, in Farsi. Then I told the man that the passport-control officer could not do this because he does not speak Farsi.

Everyone calmed down and we drank coffee and discussed the family's situation. One of the girls started to cry because she was scared and her mother had to comfort her to make her stop. The family want to stay in France, but it was not allowed. Eventually it was decided that the family would be returned to Rome, where they had just come from.

I did not think that Italy would allow the family through its border, but sending them meant that they once again became a problem for the Italian authorities, and not for the French authorities. This made the French authorities very happy.

'*Kheyli mamnum.*'

The man thanked me very much, but I do not think I was of much help to him.

The passport-control officer made me sign a form and then gave me some money to pay for my services as a translator. With the money I already had, this gave me enough to buy an economy air ticket to London.

15th November 1988

Today I arrived at Heathrow airport on flight BA288. However, things did not go well for me. Although I explained my own situation at passport control, and although I told them that my documentation had been stolen, they would not let me enter the country. They said that nothing had changed since the last time I was refused entry to the country.

They took me to a room away from the public areas and said they were going to send me back to Paris and gave me a Home Office Immigration Service Notice of Refusal of Leave to Enter.

This is what it said:

To ALFRED MEHRAN also known as NASSERI MEHRAN KARIMI

You have asked for leave to enter the United Kingdom for settlement but you do not hold a valid national passport or other document satisfactorily establishing your identity and nationality. Furthermore you have sought entry for settlement but under the Immigration Rules you are required to have entry clearance for that purpose and you have no such entry clearance.

I therefore refuse you leave to enter the United Kingdom

A. REMOVAL I have given/propose to give
DIRECTIONS directions for your removal at 20.30
hrs, on 15-11 1988, by ship/aircraft BA
318 to (country/territory) Paris, France

B. RIGHT OF APPEAL	You are entitled to appeal against refusal of leave to enter but only after you have left the United Kingdom. Any such appeal will be considered by the independent appellate authorities established for the purposes of the Act
C. HOW TO APPEAL	If you decide to appeal you should complete the attached form, IS 87, and return it to HM Inspector at the above address, to arrive not later than 28 days after your departure from the United Kingdom

When I returned to Terminal One in Charles de Gaulle airport, Burger King was already shut so I could not buy a coffee or any food. They give out food on the plane, but it is not nice. The coffee is weak.

I am now sitting on a bench outside the closed Burger King, filling out the form IS 87 which they gave me while I was in England today. When I finish, I put it in an envelope, but I cannot post it tonight because the post office is closed. Tomorrow morning I will send it to England so that my appeal can begin.

I put the envelope away in my bag so it does not get lost. Then I put my bag on one end of the bench and lie down so that I can go to sleep. I do not think I should be sleeping in a public area.

19th November 1988
I am still at the airport but I have moved. I hear the lift

doors open and I quickly duck out of sight. I am hiding in one of the corridors on the tenth floor of a hotel. If someone came out of one of the three lifts that go down to the lobby and took the corridor that goes straight ahead, then they would find me. Just past room 1035, near the end of the corridor, is a bay window that juts out from the side of the hotel. If you are in the bay, people cannot see you from further down the corridor, or from inside any of the lifts when the doors are open.

There is only one room past this point so very few individuals walk past, except for the man from room 1036. And if the man from room 1036 comes past, then you can stand up and look out of the window and pretend to be watching a plane landing at the airport, so that he does not suspect you are living in the corridor at night.

The floor by the bay window is a good place to hide. I have slept here for four nights. In the daytime, I still stay in Terminal One, but I do not think I should be there at night, so when it gets dark I go outside and get on a bus.

There are free transfer buses to take passengers from the different terminals in the airport to various places. The route-two bus travels from outside Terminal One (opposite the entrance to departure hall 16) and goes to the train station where the RER trains leave to go to Paris. By the side of the station are three very tall hotels. The one nearest the station has flag-poles outside, displaying flags from different countries around the world. Each night for the last four nights I have left Terminal One and caught the route-two bus to come to this hotel.

The first evening that I came to the hotel, I went down into the basement where they have a bar and a restaurant. I sat at a table and smoked a cigarette and ordered a coffee so that I could sit there without interruption. The bar was busy with people waiting to catch flights early the next morning. Most of them were French, with a few Germans, and some British and Americans. A television in the corner was switched to a French discussion programme, with men sitting on a panel talking about the Turin Shroud; whether it is real or a fake, and whose face does it really show.

A barman gave me matches to light my cigarettes and I sat in the bar until very late – it does not close until 2:00 a.m. But then they were clearing up and stacking the chairs on top of the tables, so I had to leave. I went to the reception desk to ask for a room. I had a little money, but the woman working there did not ask me for any.

'I'm sorry, we don't have any rooms,' she said, shaking her head. 'You should try somewhere else.'

She seemed anxious for me to leave the hotel and looked over at one of the men working on the reception desk.

'I can't take a room here?'

'No.'

So I went outside to where the flagpoles are in a line, and waited for a few minutes until a coachload of people pulled up. As they went into the hotel with their suitcases and trolleys, I followed them. There were so many of them that they blocked the view of the woman at the reception desk. I walked immediately across the entrance lobby and into a lift.

I went straight up to the tenth floor because it is the top of the building, where I thought that there would be fewer people. I walked around until I found the bay-window area that was suitable for my purpose. Next morning, I returned to the terminal, where I bought a French breakfast at Burger King, and waited there. Then in the evening I went back to the hotel.

It is now 12:23 a.m. on my fourth night of sleeping in the corridor of the hotel by the bay window, and I hear the 'ding' of the lift doors opening again. I look round the corner to see if it is the man in room 1036 coming out of the lift, because if it is the man in room 1036 then I have to stand up and watch planes landing.

It is not the man in room 1036; it is the woman from the reception desk downstairs. She is peering along both corridors. I duck my head out of the way, but I think she might have seen me. The lift doors close and she is gone. I wonder what I should do.

If she saw me, then I should move, because she might come back with the manager and they will say that they have no rooms and I will have to leave. If she did not see me, and if I move when I do not need to move, then someone else might see me because I am walking about, and I will have to leave.

On the wall is an information sign in French that says: 'Emergency Procedures. In the event of a fire, please make your way to the nearest exit in a calm and orderly fashion. Your nearest emergency exit is stairwell twelve.' I read it carefully, but it is not relevant to my situation.

I decide that I should move, because if the woman from the reception desk comes back and finds me I will have to leave the hotel. I walk to the lifts and press the silver button. It feels smooth against the end of my finger. As the lift makes the 'ping' noise, I wonder if the doors will open and the woman will be inside. It is too late to hide; the only place you can hide out of sight is by the bay window, and that is too far away to reach before the doors open.

The doors slide apart and inside the lift is the man from room 1036. He smells of smoke and beer.

'*Bonsoir, Monsieur.*'

I step into the lift and descend to the fifth floor. I wait there, standing at the end of the corridor. But it is not a good place to be because it is easy to see me if anyone comes into the corridor. I wait one hour and then I call the lift again to go back upstairs.

I step in and inside already are a man and a woman and a girl about ten years old. They have many bags and cases with them and they are in a state of agitation. I press the button for floor ten, but they have already pressed the button for the ground floor.

'Why can't I wait upstairs?' says the girl.

'Because the key won't work. We have to get another one and we're staying together,' says the woman. Then she makes a face. 'Everything was going swell until we came to Europe.'

We are going down to reception. I do not want to be in reception. The doors open and a crowd of people are waiting. The family push through them and dis-appear. The people get in and press the buttons they need for their floors. The doors close. There is no sign of the woman, who is probably busy on reception attending to new arrivals.

People get out of the lift as we go up and I am alone

from the eighth floor onwards. It is warm and safe in the hotel and I am tired and want to go to sleep.

The lift doors open on the tenth floor. Directly in front of them is the woman from reception. She says: 'That's him.'

Behind her is a policeman.

Diary extract
'2:18 a.m. I wake up because it is like someone has turned a light on, but they have not, but the middle of Terminal One is full of white snow that reflects the lights. There is big snowstorm. In twenty minutes maybe four or six inches of snowfall. There is no-one in airport because it is night so I can leave my possessions. I take camera and go up the stairs into the departure level. The automatic glass doors numbered 16 slide open and snow falls inside from where it was lying piled against the door. I take a photograph.'

Chapter 9

29th November 1988
I am sitting in the back of a police van which is not a good situation for me to be in.

The man opposite me is sitting with one arm hand-cuffed to the wall of the van, because a few minutes ago he tried to hit the man sitting next to me in the face. The name of the man opposite is Paul Ayers and he borrowed fifty thousand francs from the place where he worked after his boss said that it would be all right. But then he says his boss changed his mind, said he could not borrow the money and called the police.

The man sitting next to me is called Kibria Hussain. Kibria Hussain is from Bangladesh and has been arrested and found guilty of being in France illegally because he does not have the correct documentation. Kibria is tall and skinny. I think he is too thin. When he is allowed to (not now), he makes roll-up cigarettes and smokes them. His ambition is to become a singer and I do not think the cigarettes will be good for his voice.

Paul Ayers said that he thought he should not be sent to prison because he was not a criminal. Kibria Hussain said that if Paul Ayers did not want to go to prison then he should not have stolen fifty thousand francs from his boss. That is when Paul tried to hit him.

I hear the driver start up the engine and the van jerks forward a few feet. We wait while other guards open the big doors that lead out into the street. When the doors are open, we move forward. The seats are along each side of the van, so that two rows of prisoners sit facing each other. When the van goes round a corner, you have to put your foot out to stop yourself falling off your seat. It is not a nice way to travel.

Passengers are reminded to keep their personal baggage with them at all times.

I have been found guilty of being an illegal immigrant in France. When I was arrested at the hotel, I was taken to the police station and there I was asked for my documentation. I did not have the correct documentation and so I had to stay in jail. A judge has just said that I must go to prison.

The van is taking us to Fleury-Merogis which is the biggest prison in the whole of Europe and is where the French courts send asylum-seekers, illegal immigrants and foreign citizens who are waiting for deportation back to their country of origin. Less than half the people in the prison are French people from France. I have not been sentenced for deportation because the judge said that Iran is an unsafe country for me.

After an hour of driving, the van slows down, twisting and turning on the smaller country roads. We enter inside the gates and the van comes to a stop.

'This is the worst stinking place in the whole of France,' says a fat man at the end of the row. It is the first time that he has spoken during the entire journey. 'The courtyard stinks of shit.'

The fat man is a car thief. He is forty-two years old and has spent fifteen years out of the last twenty years in prison. When he is released, he always returns to jail.

The guards open the back of the van, uncuff Paul Ayers and then walk us from the back of the police van into the reception area. We wait for a long time. No-one is in a hurry to get anything done. We are called one by one and have to sign a form and receive a prison uniform to wear.

On one wall of the reception area is a photograph of the prison taken from high in the air, in a plane or perhaps in a helicopter. The prison looks like a huge concrete snowflake that has been built on the ground. In Fleury-Merogis prison everything is designed to be visible to the guards from the centre of the prison so bad things cannot happen without the guards knowing.

There are over six thousand prisoners in the jail but there are only three thousand cells, so everyone has to share. You have to go to the toilet in front of your cell-mate which is something that I do not like to do.

The prison officer is looking down his list.

'You two, cell 23, block C.'

I am put into a cell with Paul Ayers, which I do not mind because he does not cause any problems if you do not say things to him that are unwise.

We walk into the cell and the guard pulls shut the door behind us, making a clanging sound which shakes the room and I remember a different prison in a different country.

Paul sits on the lower bunk and begins to cry.

15th September 1965

I am standing on the bow of a boat sailing out into the Strait of Hormoz at the southern end of the Persian Gulf. I am twenty years old and the sun is shining on my face. The boat is rocking with the waves that hit the stern.

The Strait of Hormoz is the location where the Persian Gulf meets the Indian Ocean. In the middle of summer, the scorching sun and the high humidity make the climate difficult to bear. The temperature can reach 123°F (50.5°C) and, because of this, people from Tehran who are sent by their company to be employed in the Gulf will receive higher wages than others doing the same job in Tehran. In the autumn and early winter, however, the weather can be very pleasant and it is the best time to visit.

Behind us is the port of Bandar where we boarded our ferry, and ahead of us across the blue water is

Hormoz Island, a small round island about 14km in diameter. Stepping off a boat onto Hormoz Island is like travelling back in time twenty years. I turn around and see my father just behind me, watching me. He smiles. We have made this journey together before, when I was a boy.

Through the rippling heat haze I see an oil tanker slowly creeping into view, and then becoming larger and larger on the horizon, like a building sailing through the water. At least, I think I remember the oil tanker. I am not sure when I saw the oil tanker, and when I remember things again this time there is no tanker.

Straight ahead of the ferry, Hormoz Island is also getting bigger. To the north of the beach is Portuguese Castle, a huge colonial fortress finished by its Portuguese builders in 1515. My father brought me here when I was a child, and a man turned a key for us and we saw a secret that was very beautiful.

Last time we made this journey to the island my father whispered to me, 'When you have not seen the sea for a long time, then think of this moment.'

1st December 1988

Days in prison are very boring because they are always the same. I am woken at 7:00 a.m., and at 7:30 the cell door is unlocked and I leave the cell to go to the refectory to eat breakfast. If you have been prescribed any special medicines then you might get them now, but I have not been prescribed any special medicines so I do not get any.

At 8:15 a.m. some prisoners might take exercise in the prison courtyard. But usually the guards are too busy to let the prisoners out and to watch them. I do not mind not going outside because the courtyard is very unfriendly, and in many places people have used it for a toilet which I do not like.

At 9:00 a.m. I am supposed to go into the showers, but this does not happen often. One reason is because again the guards do not have the time to watch prisoners, to make sure that bad things are not happening. The second reason is that many of the showers are broken down. In my section there are two hundred prisoners using ten shower cubicles.

There is a common room where I can go, but mostly I spend my time in my cell because I do not want to cause any trouble. I will be able to leave this place sooner if I am not involved in any trouble. Also I do not like to be hit.

At 11:35 it is time to go back to the refectory for lunch. The staff have their meal between 12:30–1:30, and so I must have my meal and be back locked inside my cell by that time.

From 1:30 p.m. I am either given a book and locked in my cell, or occasionally I am sent out for some exercise in the courtyard. If there is a hearing to go to because someone is in trouble, then that will be held in the afternoon. There is also a large workshop where some prisoners can get a job if they behave well and then they can earn extra money for cigarettes.

At 4:30 a trolley goes around, which is a delivery service like a corner shop, and people are given anything that they have ordered from the prison canteen. I can order from a leaflet by ticking boxes if I want to buy something. I have to use a black pen to tick the boxes; I am not allowed to use a pencil. But it does not matter because I have no money to buy things anyway.

I go back to the refectory again at 5:45 p.m. for dinner, and at 6:45 I return to the cell and I am locked inside for twelve hours overnight.

Every day is exactly the same.

3rd December 1988

I am now alone in the cell. Two days ago, Paul Ayers got into a fight in the refectory at lunchtime. Someone pushed him from behind and he pushed them back, and soon there was a conflict. As punishment, he was put into the segregation block of the prison in a small cell in solitary confinement. He is not allowed to see any other prisoners or to have any privileges. Every hour, the guards go along the cells in the solitary confinement area and check the prisoners inside by looking through the eyepiece on the door. A guard can look in, but a prisoner cannot look out. I do not know when they will let him out.

I am sitting on my bed reading a newspaper when Kibria calls me through the cell door. He comes inside looking very happy.

'I am getting out! My lawyers appealed against my sentence and they have accepted some new documents, so I am leaving. Today. In a few hours.'

I tell him congratulations, it is good news.

'I brought your book back.'

He hands me back the copy of *Far from Home* by American writer Walter Tevis, which I had lent him to read. Then he gives me his packet of papers and tobacco that he uses to make his roll-up cigarettes.

'It is not my brand,' I tell him, but he says to take it anyway and to trade it if I do not want it. So I take it.

'I can get on with my music,' Kibria says.

He has ambitions to be a pop musician on television like Madonna or Elton John. I wish him good luck and he shakes my hand and leaves because he wants to tell other people his good news. I do not see him again. I put the book Kibria has returned on Paul Ayers's bed, next to a pile of three old newspapers.

In the night there is much noise. Inmates are banging plastic trays against the door of their cell. They are all banging together, in time. The rhythm gets faster and faster until they are just smashing the trays into the doors as quickly as they can, then they stop and start again with a slow beat.

It is very hard to sleep and I am glad that Kibria is not here any more. I wonder if he is in Charles de Gaulle airport, Terminal One, sitting on my bench near Burger King, but such an occurrence is unlikely.

In the morning, the guard unlocks the door of the cell and waits in the doorway. This is very unusual. He waits until I sit up and then he comes inside. He tells me some news.

'Last night, when his cell was checked at 3.00 a.m. the guard found that Paul Ayers had hung himself. He used a length of cloth that he'd tied to one of the bars on the window, and then kicked away the chair he was standing on. You'll be getting a new cellmate.'

Paul is the third person to commit suicide in Fleury-Merogis in the last month. Each of them was a hanging. One man hung himself with his own boot-laces. Later that day, many prisoners refuse to go back into their cells as a protest against the conditions in the prison.

I move the books and the three newspapers off Paul Ayers's bed. It is not correct to keep them there in the current situation.

Diary extract
'3 p.m. I took a photograph of pieces of paper on the floor that looked like small pieces of paper from a wedding. Someone had left a suitcase in the corridor by the Lost & Found and it was security risk. So the woman in the dry-cleaning shop called the bomb squad and they came. First they make dog smell suitcase and then they touch suitcase with metal pole. Everyone else had to leave the area but I did not leave because I am a special case and because I have nowhere else to go. So man with plastic shield stood in front of my table in case of dangerous impact.

Finally they plant their own explosive next to case and blow it up because they believed that inside the suitcase was a bomb. But inside the suitcase was not a bomb only clothes and papers belonging to a passenger named Bek Bekir who was travelling from Turkey to London. Pieces of paper were scattered all over corridor and before anyone cleaned it up I took a photograph with my camera. Very pretty.'

Chapter 10

15th January 1989
I was released from Fleury-Merogis prison two days

ago. They gave me back my shoulder bag and my clothes and also gave me a piece of paper that said I had to leave France within forty-eight hours. But I cannot leave France because I have no passport or documents so no country will let me cross their border.

The closest I can get to England is Terminal One in Charles de Gaulle airport. I am less likely to be arrested inside the airport than if I am outside and also perhaps I can save enough money for a ticket to go to United Kingdom. So when I was released from Fleury-Merogis, I made my way back to Terminal One as quickly as I could travel. I had to walk into the town and wait at a bus shelter for a bus to Paris, then take the RER to Gare du Nord again, and then change lines to arrive at the airport.

When I got there, a young woman wearing a long black skirt was sitting on my bench by the Burger King. She was reading a book titled *Stolz und Vorurteil* and did not look up very often. I waited, and soon she had to leave to catch her plane which was the 15:33 flight 423 to Berlin. As soon as she moved, I quickly sat on the red bench, which is my proper place.

This morning I went to the post office downstairs on the boutique level to see if there was any mail for me. People there understand my situation. I have no regular address so I use: Sir Alfred Mehran, c/o Post Office, Boutique Level, Charles de Gaulle Airport, Paris.

'c/o' means 'care of' and that means that although I do not live inside the post office because they will not permit such a thing, they will keep important official replies from British authorities for me so that I can receive them.

While I had been away in prison a letter had arrived from the British Embassy, concerning my documentation. The letter said:

Mr Alfred MEHRAN
Poste Restante
Annexe 1, Aerogare No 1
Charles de Gaulle
95711 Roissy

09 January 1989

Dear Sir

When you enquired here last week about your outstanding appeal following the refusal by the Immigration Officer at Heathrow Airport to allow you to enter the United Kingdom on 15.11.88 (you had no travel document), we undertook to make enquiries on your behalf.

This we have now done, and it appears that your appeal has gone forward to the appropriate authorities to take its turn in the queue for a hearing. Due to extreme pressure of work, it is understood this is likely to take a year, or even longer!

Under the circumstances, you may consider it prudent to endeavour to obtain a passport from your own embassy in Paris or, alternatively, to seek advice from the United Nations High Commissioner for Refugees, 159 avenue Charles de Gaulle, 92200 Neuilly-sur-Seine.

I regret that we can be of no further assistance in this matter, and any future enquiries regarding your appeal should be directed to the UK Immigration Authorities whose address and telephone number are on the form IS131 in your possession.

Yours faithfully

Visa Section

So I must wait here at Terminal One in Charles de Gaulle airport for up to one year while they deal with my application.

The machine that cooks the French fries in Burger King was broken today; they could not sell any French fries and nobody could buy any French fries either. They said an engineer is coming to fix it soon.

18th January 1989
After three days the machine that makes the French fries in Burger King is working once again.

18th February 1989
Everyone says I must write to a man named Christian Bourguet. This is why:

A few days ago I was arrested once again. I cannot describe exact circumstances because they are very distressing, but I have been arrested for being an illegal person in France with no documentation. I have not been out of prison for very long and already I am arrested again. This is very bad for me. When I go to court again, if the judge finds me guilty I will be sent to prison for a longer period of time.

I do not think this is fair: I cannot leave France to go to another country because I have no passport, so no other country will accept me; but when I stay in France I am arrested for being illegal, although there is nowhere else that I can go.

Many people have told me about Christian Bourguet and that he can help me in my situation. Monsieur Bourguet is a French human rights lawyer who works in Paris. He is a specialist in the problems of refugees and asylum-seekers.

He grew up in Maroc and Algiers and has a special interest in Islamic culture, partly because of where he grew up and partly because his father also had a special interest in the same subject. He is a member of GISTI, a group who provide information and support to immigrants.

I have spoken to several people who have been represented by Monsieur Bourguet and they say that he has helped them very much.

He has been at the centre of some famous cases as well. For example, Monsieur Bourguet was involved in trying to end the Iranian Hostage Crisis, when the Iranians seized the American Embassy and held many people captive, starting in November 1979.

Mr Bourguet acted as a negotiator for the Iranian government, together with François Cheron, another human rights lawyer, and an Argentinian business-man, Hector Villalon.

To solve the crisis between Iran and America, the new Iranian minister of Foreign Affairs, Sadegh Ghotzadeh, asked Monsieur Bourguet and his colleagues to go to

Panama in South America to negotiate the Shah's extradition back to Iran in return for the release of the hostages. They did this and worked very hard, but the negotiations did not bring about a solution.

I have been given Monsieur Bourguet's address so I sit down and write him a letter outlining my situation, asking him to represent me when I appear in court charged with being an illegal person. I explain that I have no money to pay him and that the court appearance is in two days' time. I hope he will agree.

21st February 1989

I am in court. Monsieur Bourguet has accepted my case but he cannot be here today because he has another court date. He has sent his junior partner to represent me, but she knows nothing of my story or the history of Iran and so I am found guilty and sentenced to time in prison. I am taken outside and placed in a police van and driven to Fleury-Merogis prison. I know the journey very well. For me, this result is not good.

In my diary for 12th April I wrote this:
'This morning I thought someone was going to hit me in the face with a breakfast tray. But they did not. They hit the person next to me, because when I saw they were going to hit me I moved out of the way very quickly. There is more fighting than last time I was here. People hate this place, but they make trouble so they have to stay longer.

23rd May 1989

The sun is on my face. At the table next to me, a small

boy is complaining because his boat has sunk and his mother would not let him climb into the boating lake to rescue it. He is not allowed to go in because, although he can take off his shoes and socks, his trousers would still get wet and this occurrence is something that his mother is keen to avoid. The boy's name is Philip. I do not know his mother's name because he calls her 'Mama'.

I am sitting in the open-air café in the Jardin du Luxembourg in the middle of the Left Bank in Paris. The Jardin du Luxembourg is supposed to be the most popular park in Paris because it is so beautiful. It is not very crowded today because it is the middle of the afternoon and most people are working. Men are sitting on green metal chairs, playing chess in the shade of the chestnut trees.

The boy is still complaining about losing his boat in the Octagonal Lake and his mother agrees to buy him an ice cream. I think she agrees to this to make him become quiet. I drink my espresso and sit and feel the sun on my face. I have not felt the sun for a long time.

When I was released from Fleury-Merogis prison again, they gave me a piece of paper that said I had to leave France within forty-eight hours again. But I did not do this because I still have nowhere to go that will accept me. Instead I came to Paris to see my lawyer and ask him why he did not come to represent me. I finish my espresso and then I walk to the offices of Monsieur Bourguet which are nearby.

I tell the lady in the office outside that I do not have an appointment with Monsieur Bourguet and she looks quite surprised. She disappears, and when she comes back she says that Monsieur Bourguet will see me now, which seems to surprise her even more.

She shows me into his office. Monsieur Bourguet is a tall man with black hair and a well kept beard. To me, he looks like a diplomat.

'Monsieur Mehran.'

We shake hands.

I tell him that I have just come from Fleury-Merogis prison where I had to spend time because he did not come and represent me; instead he sent his junior partner who knows nothing about Iran and did not understand my story, and so I was sent to jail.

'Please, tell me your story,' says Monsieur Bourguet. He takes out his pipe. 'I am ready to hear it.'

So while Monsieur Bourguet smokes his pipe, I relate my story: how I left my home and went to the University of Bradford in England; how the money stopped coming; how I returned to Iran; how I was arrested; how I was released; how I went to England and claimed asylum; how they refused; and how I was refused asylum in Netherlands, Italy, Germany and France. And finally, how I came to Charles de Gaulle airport without my passport and got on a plane to England, and how they sent me back.

'What happened to your original passport? The one you had when they expelled you from Iran,' Christian asks me.

I tell him this.

7th August 1987

I am at Gare du Nord standing on the RER platform waiting for the B3 train to Charles de Gaulle airport. I am wearing light trousers, a short-sleeved shirt, and

I am carrying a shoulder bag that contains everything I own in the world.

The streets are full of sweating tourists. Deep under Gare du Nord the tunnels feel like an oven. An overweight woman sits down on the plastic seats and mops her forehead. A section of platform recently repaired with black pitch oozes under my feet.

'Excusez-moi. Pouvez-vous m'aider?'

A man is speaking to me. He is tall and thin and unshaven. I open my mouth to tell him that I do not speak French, when I feel another man grab the strap of my bag. He rips it from my shoulder with both hands. The first man that spoke to me pushes me in the chest and knocks me off balance, so I fall back onto the platform. I turn my head and see the man with the bag running along the platform towards an exit staircase. The man who pushed me is running after him. They are thieves working together. They have taken everything.

After an hour of searching, I see my bag sticking out of a litter bin three levels up, on the D platform for trains heading north to Orry-la-Ville. Inside is a paperback book, but everything else has vanished. Although it will be no use to the thieves, they have taken my documentation. My refugee papers are gone.

The top of my bag is smeared with a mouldy banana skin from the bin. The banana skin is mashed into the metal teeth of the zipper. I start to wipe it off, but it just makes more mess.

23rd May 1989

While I talk, Monsieur Bourguet lights his pipe, inhales, then lets it go out and relights it again. He listens patiently to my story. Occasionally he asks a question, and even more occasionally he makes a note of a date or a name, but mostly he just listens. I like him.

At the end of my story, Monsieur Bourguet takes a deep drag on his pipe and says, 'I will take your case. I will do the preparation to lodge a claim for homeless status.'

This is a good result for me. I like Monsieur Bourguet and I think he is a very good lawyer. On the wall to the left of Monsieur Bourguet's desk is a framed picture of US President Jimmy Carter. Next to the picture is a typed letter. Monsieur Bourguet sees me looking at it, gets up and takes it off the wall to show me. The letter says:

The White House
March 12, 1980

To Christian Bourguet,
I hope you will accept my personal thanks and appreciation for your untiring efforts to peacefully resolve the crisis which presently exists between the United States and Iran. The personal courage and perseverance that you have demonstrated in this effort have been an inspiration to everyone here.

We share your own disappointment that our recent efforts were not successful, but I believe that we have made progress. I will not rest until our hostages are released and this crisis resolved, and I hope that you will continue to be a partner in this effort.
Sincerely,
Jimmy Carter

At the bottom of the letter is the signature of the President of the United States. Next to it is another letter. This one is handwritten and the notepaper is headed 'Air Force One'.

'That one was written on the President's aeroplane as he was flying from the USA to Germany to meet the hostages when they had been released,' Monsieur Bourguet tells me.

He puts the picture back on the wall again and we sit down. There is a third letter from the President but I cannot read it for two reasons. First, I cannot see it from where I am now sitting, even if I screw my eyes up quite tightly and concentrate. The second reason is that the letter does not concern me, and if I read it I may look as if I am a very nosey individual.

'Do you have a place to stay where I can get in touch with you?' Monsieur Bourguet asks me.

'Yes,' I tell him.

He picks up a pen to write down the location.

'What is the address?'

'Terminal One, Charles de Gaulle Airport.'

Monsieur Bourguet smiles. I do not know why.

Diary extract
'11:35 p.m. I saw worker from Lufthansa airline. He came to my bench and gave me Lufthansa luggage box that he knew I wanted because I had asked him for one. Luggage box is perfect size for keeping newspapers and magazines safe so that they are not lost or stolen. I have a trolley now so I can keep newspaper in Lufthansa luggage box on trolley and move around on departure level or boutique level.'

Chapter 11

10th August 1989
I am sitting on my bench near Burger King in Terminal One of Charles de Gaulle airport talking to my lawyer, Monsieur Bourguet. Monsieur Bourguet has agreed to take on my case and help me get my proper documentation from the French authorities so that I can stay in France without being arrested and sent to jail.

Monsieur Bourguet has begun writing letters to many organizations who can help provide evidence that I should be allowed to stay without arrest.

Today he has shown me a letter from the British Embassy about my situation. This is what the letter said:

British Embassy
Consular Section rue Joseph II 28
1040 Brussels

to
N Stewart Esq
Consular Section
British Embassy
Paris

Our Ref 2055/89

Date 10th July 1989

Dear Colleague

MEHRAN KARIMI NASSERI AKA ALFRED MEHRAN – 19.11.1945

1. I refer to your letter of 22 June about the above named.

2. Mr Karimi is well known at this office. In fact we were wondering what had happened to him as he used to visit us weekly, not always for a specific reason. He has, as you might guess, a long immigration history: either by travelling to the United Kingdom without a visa or being refused one at this office. He always appeals. I enclose some copies of correspondence to give you a little background information, including a letter from the UKIAS advising Mr Karimi not to

keep on travelling to the United Kingdom!
(Annex A)

3. Concerning his 'statelessness' and his claim
that this office has documentary evidence on
this subject: in 1985 he was in trouble with the
Belgian authorities as he refused to register
with the local commune as required by Belgian
law. The Belgian authorities were willing to
register him but Mr Karimi considered he did
not wish to be resident in the country.
Whenever he was picked up for an identity
check, he was kept overnight by the police
until they could check his identity with the
Ministry of Justice as Mr Karimi had no valid
documents. My predecessor gave Mr Karimi a
letter stating that he (mr [sic] Karimi) had
applied for a United Kingdom visa, which had
been refused and that he was now awaiting the
outcome of his appeal (Annex B). My predecessor described Mr Karimi as *'apatride'* and
since then Mr Karimi has maintained that as
this office conferred statelessness upon him we
were therefore responsible for him.

Yours ever,
[signature]
P.J. Arn (Mrs)

Of course, *'apatride'* is a French word meaning
'stateless person'.

Monsieur Bourguet says that there may be a chance
to claim that I have been British citizen all my life
which would mean that I would be accepted straight

119

away as a British citizen. This is because of what the British said when the Prime Minister of Iran, Dr Mossadeq, nationalized the Anglo-Oil Company in 1951.

The British wanted to go to the International Court to ask them to condemn Iran for breaking the law. They could not do this because that court is not for problems between countries and private companies, but for problems between two countries. The area around Masjed Soleiman contained many refineries and oilfields which the Shah had allowed to be protected by British forces since the First World War, so the British tried to claim that the area was a colony of the British Empire. The court did not accept their argument and they lost.

Monsieur Bourguet has told me that perhaps we can use the fact that the British claimed that the area was a British colony to claim that therefore I am a British citizen, or at least a citizen of the Commonwealth. If that does not work, then Monsieur Bourguet says he will lodge a claim for homeless status.

I hope it will not be long before there is an answer to my problem. I will wait for my solution inside Terminal One, Charles de Gaulle airport because outside the airport the risk of arrest for being illegal is much greater. Inside the airport people leave me alone.

12th January 1990
This morning at 10:15 a.m. Dr Bargain visited me. He works at the airport's medical centre on the boutique level of Terminal One.

Dr Bargain usually wears a bow tie; today it is a

blue one with small pink spots. He is a small man with greying temples and glasses. He has a big smile and laughs often and makes many jokes. Today, the hair from one of his nostrils is coming out more than the hair from the other nostril, but I do not say anything because it would be impolite.

Dr Bargain comes to talk to me quite often, maybe once a week. He asks me if I have voucher for food and if I am feeling well. I told him that if I drink too much coffee then I do not sleep well. I am sleeping on bench near Burger King and sometimes I get woken up by people walking around, or by shadows.

'How much coffee do you drink, Alfred?'

'Five, maybe six espresso every day.'

Dr Bargain laughs.

Once when we were sitting on my bench, Dr Bargain said to me, 'Alfred, your father was a doctor with a medical practice, and my father was also a doctor with a medical practice. We are both sons of doctors.'

I said, 'Yes,' because it is true. I do not know why he says something that is a fact we both already know.

Dr Philippe Bargain has worked in the airport since 1974 and is now the head of the medical services. He told me that each day they have two doctors, three nurses, two drivers of the ambulances, and a secretary inside the medical centre.

They deal with many things, from passengers who have heart attacks, to when there is a catastrophe, such as a plane crash. Many strange things, too.

'Alfred, do you know what I have just been doing? Just now?' says Dr Bargain.

'No.'

'At 7 a.m., the airport police brought a man to the medical centre. They thought that he was hiding drugs inside his body, so they wanted us to X-ray him to find out.'

'Did you do it?'

'Yes, of course. The police bring people to be X-rayed perhaps one hundred times a year. We took an X-ray, developed it, and inside his stomach we saw a bag with maybe two or three kilos of drugs. The police took him to jail.'

'Did he swallow the bag?'

'Yes, he swallowed it. How else would it get there, Alfred? The first year that I became chief of the medical service, a person did the exact same thing – he swallowed some drugs to try and smuggle them through customs. But the bag burst in his stomach during the in-flight meal, while they were still in the air. The medical centre received a call from the control tower and I had to rush out to the runway to meet the plane.'

'Did you pump his stomach so it was empty?'

'No, I went up the steps onto the plane as soon as I could when it landed, but the man was already dead. He should have put the drugs in a better bag.'

18th February 1990

I am being interviewed by a woman from a television station. I have never been interviewed for television before. So I have shaved and tried to look good. Monsieur Bourguet says that it might help my situation if someone makes a television interview about me.

Last year, in the summer, a woman rang my lawyer,

Monsieur Bourguet, and asked him if he knew of any interesting stories. She wanted to write a piece for a monthly magazine called *J'accuse* (like the book by Zola), which is a magazine about what happens in the French legal system and courts. So Monsieur Bourguet told her my story; she wrote a piece and they published it. I did not see a copy because they do not sell this magazine at the newsagent in Terminal One.

Two months later, the same woman called Monsieur Bourguet on the telephone and said that a television channel was interested in my situation and can she make a television report with me. Monsieur Bourguet said I should do it because it might help my case.

The woman was supposed to come at 10 a.m., but she arrived at 11:15 a.m. This does not matter to me because I am always here, sitting on my bench by Burger King. But if someone says they will arrive at a certain time, then they really ought to arrive at that time even if it does not matter to me.

With the woman reporter came a cameraman and a sound engineer. They set up their equipment, lights and microphone, so that they can film the interview. She asks me to stand in front of the camera and lights so that the cameraman can hold up an exposure meter to my face. An exposure meter is a device which registers if there is enough light on my face to make a television interview.

'*Oui, très bien.*'

We do a sound test which is also positive.

The lady journalist stands in front of the camera and speaks an introduction to explain that my situation is the situation of a man who does not have the correct documentation.

'Now, I am going to ask you some questions and Alfred, you just answer them as if you are just talking to me, OK?'

I say, '*Je comprends.*'

'*Trois, deux, un* . . .'

I see a policeman coming towards us. He is looking at the television lights.

'*Pardon* . . .' The lady tells the cameraman to stop filming.

'What are you doing here?' asks the policeman.

'We're shooting a news piece for television.'

The policeman looks around at the lights and the microphone.

'This is a public airport. It is forbidden to film here,' says the policeman.

The lady journalist quickly looks in her handbag, takes out a white envelope and unfolds a letter.

'We have authorization from the airport authorities.'

The policeman reads the letter. I help him by pointing to the letter while he holds it.

'And who is this man? Can I see your papers, *s'il vous plaît, Monsieur*?'

Passengers are reminded to keep their personal baggage with them at all times.

I shrug my shoulders. 'I have no papers. They are filming me because I am stuck here at Terminal One, Charles de Gaulle airport, because I have no papers,' I explain.

'If you have no papers, Monsieur, then you will have to come with me. *Allons-y*. You are under arrest.'

124

The lady journalist begins to argue with the policeman, which only makes him more upset. He says that I have to go with him to the police centre in the airport.

I go with him.

Instead of making a television interview about my situation of not having the correct documentation, I am arrested for being in the situation of not having the correct documentation. For me this is not a good result.

Diary extract
'Dr Bargain visited me this morning. He asked if my electric razor was working. I said, "Yes. It's working." Dr Bargain had taken away the batteries from my razor and recharged them in twenty-four hours. The razor is working well, and it doesn't give the red-light signal on the side any more. Yesterday I shaved three times to ensure good presentation.'

Chapter 12

20th March 1990
After I am arrested many things happen.

The lady journalist calls Monsieur Bourguet on the telephone and explains what has happened. She says she is very sorry for what has occurred because it was her fault. This is an opinion that I entirely agree with. Monsieur Bourguet tells the lady journalist that it was not her fault. This is an opinion that I do not entirely agree with.

The lady journalist asks if she can do anything to help and my lawyer suggests two things.

The first thing is for her to go to court this afternoon, when I am appearing, and ask for a postponement. The court has to agree to this if my lawyer cannot be in attendance.

Secondly, Monsieur Bourguet asks her to tell everyone that she knows – in television, the national press, radio, the regional press – about my situation, and what happened on 18th February. The lady journalist agrees to do this.

I cannot go back to Terminal One, Charles de Gaulle airport, because I have to stay in jail for one month until my case is heard. Monsieur Bourguet begins to prepare my defence.

Eight days later, Monsieur Bourguet receives a very unusual phone call.

'You don't know me but I know you,' says the person calling Monsieur Bourguet. 'I am the head of the border police in Charles de Gaulle airport. I am calling you to propose a deal.'

Monsieur Bourguet tells me he thought this was very strange, but he said, 'What is your deal?'

'You want freedom for your client, Alfred Mehran? If you stop all this publicity about the case, then he will be released in two days.'

Monsieur Bourguet tells me that he was very surprised because this is not normally how things proceed. But he agreed the deal. Then he spoke to the lady journalist and asked her to stop all the reports and the publicity in the media. He told her that if they do not keep to the deal, then she can make a new report exposing the fact that they broke their promise.

Before Monsieur Bourguet has time to even send a letter to the court asking them to release me from jail, he receives another phone call. This one is from the court, saying that tomorrow they will answer his demand to free me.

The next day, Monsieur Bourguet goes to the court. Before he can make any appeal, the prosecutor says, 'Mr Mehran has asked for freedom and we accept.'

This means that I am still charged with being in France illegally and without the correct documentation, but that I do not have to stay in jail while I wait for the case to go to court. I do not want to stay in jail.

'Alfred, they are releasing you "under control", which means that you have to go to the police station every week to prove that you are still here. You have to give an address where you can be reached,' Monsieur Bourguet explains.

'Do you have an address?' asks the prosecutor.

'Yes,' I say.

'What is it?'

'Bench by Burger King, ground level, Charles de Gaulle airport.'

The prosecutor says it is impossible to accept this as my address. He says it is an address for commerce and banks and restaurants, but not for people.

'Perhaps you could put down my office as his address?' says Monsieur Bourguet, but they will not accept it because they say I could not live in Monsieur Bourguet's office for three weeks. Which is true, because I prefer to return to Charles de Gaulle airport.

Then at the back of the court, a man who I have never seen before raises his hand.

'May I say something?'

'*Oui, Monsieur*. Who are you?' asks the judge.

The man shows his ID card. 'I am a police officer from Charles de Gaulle airport and I've been sent here by my chief. I have a house within the jurisdiction of this court and he can live there if he likes.'

So the judge accepts this because the man is a policeman. Now I have to go and live in the house of a policeman who I have never seen before.

10th April 1990

I do not stay in the policeman's house long. I stay only eight days, then I return to Terminal One, Charles de Gaulle airport. This time when I return, there is no-one sitting on my bench near Burger King. I did not have to wait to sit down on my bench; I can sit down immediately.

After the judge decided that I should live in the house of the policeman, Monsieur Bourguet gave the judge a written defence explaining my position. The judge said that because my case was very complex, the court would render its decision after one month.

After one month I returned to the court once more. The judge decided that I am guilty of staying illegally in France, but that whether I will be sent to prison or not will not be decided for six months.

This is a part of the judgement of the court:

TRIBUNAL DE GRANDE INSTANCE
93 BOBIGNY

17th Chamber   JUDGEMENT IN CRIMINAL
                      CASE

NATURE OF THE OFFENCE: ILLEGAL ENTRY OR
RESIDENCE OF A FOREIGNER IN FRANCE

HEARING 20TH   SENTENCE PASSED 20TH
March 1990   March 1990

SUBMITTED TO THE COURT:	ORDER of the judge delegated by application of article 396 of the Penal Code. JUDGEMENT GIVEN AFTER DUE HEARING OF THE PARTIES dated 20th FEBRUARY 1990, ordering the referral of the case to the hearing of 20th March 1990.

THE ACCUSED

NAME	MEHRAN ALFRED ALIAS
FIRST NAMES	Karimi Nasseri
Age at time of alleged offence	45
Date	Born 19th November 1945
and place of birth	99 MASJED-SOLEIMAN IRAN
Paternal descent	Son of Abdulkarim
Maternal descent	and Simone...
Profession	NONE
Domicile	NO FIXED ABODE
Nationality	IRANIAN
Marital status	BACHELOR
Military status	UNKNOWN
Previous record	Previous conviction
Security measure	Warrant issued on 18th FEBRUARY 1990 by Mme PRAGER, judge appointed by the President of the Court – bailed and placed on probation on 2nd March 1990.
Appearance in court	Appeared in court, assisted by Maître Christian BOURGUET, barrister-at-law, PARIS B 452 and M. Sid. ROUIS, sworn interpreter

HEARING PROCEEDINGS

On 18th FEBRUARY 1990, ALFRED MEHRAN ALIAS
Karimi Nasseri was brought before the delegated judge in
accordance with regular court procedure, as set out in
articles 388, 393, 395 and 396 of the Penal Code, before the
court on suspicion:

OF HAVING, AT ROISSY CHARLES DE GAULLE, ON
17TH FEBRUARY 1990, AS A FOREIGNER STAYED IN
METROPOLITAN FRANCE, IN CONTRAVENTION OF
BOTH ARTICLES 5 AND 6 OF REGULATION 45-2658
OF 2ND NOVEMBER 1945, INTERNATIONAL TREATIES
AND AGREEMENTS, AND IN VIOLATION OF
TERRITORIAL PROHIBITION.

Acts set out and declared illegal by ART. 19 Al. 1, 5, 6
REGULATION 45-2658 OF 2.11.1945

After questioning, MEHRAN ALFRED ALIAS Karimi
Nasseri was remanded in custody and placed under a
warrant of confinement.
As no court hearing could be held that day, the accused
was brought before the 17th chamber for a hearing at 1.00
on 20 FEBRUARY 1990.
At the aforementioned session, since the court did not
have sufficient evidence to rule on the matter, the case was
postponed after due hearing of the parties until 20th
MARCH 1990, the Court having ordered that MEHRAN
ALFRED ALIAS Karimi Nasseri be kept in custody.
In a request dated 28th February 1990, MEHRAN
ALFRED ALIAS Karimi Nasseri asked to be released on
bail. At the hearing of 2nd March 1990, the court, after due
hearing of the parties, ordered that the accused be released
on bail and placed on probation.

At this hearing, the presiding judge confirmed the identity of MEHRAN ALFRED ALIAS Karimi Nasseri, then informed the court of the events leading to legal proceedings.

MEHRAN ALFRED ALIAS Karimi Nasseri was questioned in the presence of his lawyer, Maître BOURGUET.

The summing up of the prosecution case was heard.

MEHRAN ALFRED ALIAS Karimi Nasseri presented his defence, and was the last to speak.

Maître BOURGUET's speech for the defence was heard.

The Clerk took note of the course of the proceedings.

Then the Court, after deliberation, ruled in these terms:

REASONS FOR THE JUDGEMENT

(...)

That he maintains that he is of dual English and Iranian nationality, having been born on 19th November in Masjed Soleiman (Iran) on territory that belonged to the Anglo-Iranian Oil Company until 1952, to an Iranian father and a mother whose nationality was, according to him, English;

Given that it is up to the accused to establish his status as a stateless person;

That if his British nationality has not been recognised, he cannot be considered as stateless without recognition of that status by a European authority;

That OFPRA [The French Office for the Protection of Refugees and Stateless People] has not recognised his right to that status; that the only mention in the letter from the British Consulate of 10th July 1989, giving the opinion of a person who is not a signatory of that letter, is insufficient;

Given that, although the accused claims to have been recognised as a stateless person by the High Commission for Refugees in Belgium, he provided no document to back this up;

That the court has at present no information that would allow it to grant M. Mehran the status of a stateless person rather than Iranian nationality;

That it therefore falls to the court to keep M. Mehran in custody.

FOR THESE REASONS

The court publicly ruling on criminal offences in the first instance and AFTER DUE HEARING OF THE PARTIES with regard to MEHRAN ALFRED ALIAS Karimi Nasseri, declares MEHRAN ALFRED ALIAS Karimi Nasseri guilty of the charges brought against him, and by application of the aforementioned articles.

ADJOURNS TO 26TH SEPTEMBER 1990 THE PRONUNCEMENT OF SENTENCE, in accordance with article 469-3 of the Penal Code.

Orders the production of his birth certificate and the evidence he provided to OFPRA for his status as a stateless person.

Orders the continuation of judicial supervision.

Costs reserved.
(...)

The judge said that I should bring evidence that I have lodged a claim at the French Office for Refugees and Stateless to be admitted to France as a refugee.

Monsieur Bourguet says this is wrong. The reason he thinks this is wrong is because they should not say this at the same time as finding me guilty. Either I am guilty, or I am homeless. If the FOPRA decides that I am a refugee today, then legally, Monsieur Bourguet says, I have been a refugee since I first entered France, so I cannot be guilty.

27th July 1990

I went to the newsagent today to see if they had a copy of *The Economist* and I saw a new issue of *L'Evénement du Jeudi* which I wanted to find anyway because one month ago I was interviewed by journalist from that magazine. On the cover was a colour photograph of Elizabeth Taylor and the words *'La Tragédie des Stars'*. I picked up the magazine and flicked through the pages until I found picture of myself. My interview is on a double-page spread under the heading *'Deux ans de Camping Roissy-Charles-de-Gaulle'*. There is a colour picture of me sitting on my red bench. Picture is acceptable although there is shadow on my neck. I have made other interviews but this is the first time that I have been in magazine that is sold at the airport newsagent which means it is important magazine. I show to Dr Bargain and he says he will buy his own copy.

24th August 1990

I am sitting on my bench in Terminal One of Charles de Gaulle airport. In my hand is a piece of shiny, gold-coloured cardboard that I am using as a fan because it is very hot. Terminal One has many windows and the sun can enter in many places.

I am waiting on my bench when I see Monsieur Bourguet walking towards me across the departure-hall floor.

'*Bonjour*, Alfred.'

I invite him to sit down.

'I did not come on my motorbike today. It is too hot to ride around in the sun. Don't you get too hot sitting in here?'

I tell him, no, it's not a problem. Then I make a joke and say, 'Better to be in here and be hot, than be arrested outside and be put in prison.'

Monsieur Bourguet opens his brown leather brief-case. One side has a scrape mark on it near the handle.

'Alfred, you know that I have been contacting people to find out if I can find any evidence that you should be acknowledged as a British citizen?'

I say, 'Yes'.

'I want you to read this letter.'

Monsieur Bourguet takes out a file from his brief-case, looks through it and then hands me a letter. I have to read the document to find out what it says. This is what I read:

Centre de
Service social
Brabantia
a.s.b.l.–v.z.w.
centrum voor maatschappelijk werk

> Maître De La Contrie
> Avenue de l'Observatoire, 16
> 75006 Paris
> France

> Brussels, 31 July 1990

Maître,

Following our telephone conversation, I have looked in our files for the document mentioning the British nationality of Monsieur Mehran's mother. Unfortunately, I have found no trace of it, except for a request for the birth certificate of a certain Madame SEMON(?)

I therefore regret that I cannot help you any further.

For your information, I should point out to you that Monsieur Mehran was granted refugee status by Belgium on 7.10.81.

I wish you success in your efforts to help this person. If I can be of any further assistance, please let me know.

Your sincerely

Edith Braun
Social Assistant

I finish reading the letter.

'Alfred, when I read here that you were acknowledged by Belgium as a refugee in October 1981 I
couldn't believe it,' says Monsieur Bourguet. 'You
never mentioned this to me in all our meetings and all
the times we have been in court. If Belgium has
acknowledged you as a refugee, then France will also
have to acknowledge you as a refugee.'

I shrug my shoulders. I am not familiar with the
legal situation between Belgium and France.

'So I wrote back and asked for more details.'

Monsieur Bourguet takes another letter from his file
and gives that to me to read. It says:

Centre de
Service social
Brabantia
a.s.b.l.–v.z.w.
centrum voor maatschappelijk werk

> Maître De La Contrie
> Avenue de l'Observatoire, 16
> 75006 Paris
> France

> Brussels, 16th August 1990

Maître,

In reply to your letter of 10th August, I regret to tell
you that, unfortunately, we do not possess a copy of
the request addressed to the General Register Office.

Here, however, is a very short biography of Monsieur Mehran up until the recognition of his refugee status in Belgium. The dates are imprecise, please forgive me.

- 11.74–12.75:   London (he would have had an immigration card)
- 12.75–?:   Iran
- ?–?.77:   London (request for asylum)
- ?–?:   Germany
- ?–?:   Netherlands (request for asylum – refused)
- 10.77–?.78:   France (request for asylum – refused)
- ?–?:   Italy (request for asylum – refused)
- ?–10.80:   France (appeal against the first refusal – new refusal (1.80) – request for emigration to England – several attempts to go to England – notification of expulsion on 20.08.80)
22.10.80:   crosses Belgium to go to Germany. Germany expels him.
23.10.80:   requests asylum in Belgium.

On 7.10.81, M. Mehran was recognised as a refugee by the United Nations High Commission on Refugees – 11 A, rue Van Eijek, 1050 Brussels. Tel: 02/649.01.51. His file number is c.35.220. Please find attached a copy of his refugee certificate.

Since being recognised as a refugee, M. Mehran has repeatedly attempted to travel to England.

Please feel free to contact me for further information.

Yours sincerely

Edith Braun
Social Assistant

Behind the letter is a copy of my refugee certificate from United Nations High Commissioner.

'Alfred, this is one of the documents which you lost in the mugging at Gare du Nord, yes?'

7th August 1987

Deep under Gare du Nord the tunnels feel like an oven. An overweight woman sits down on the plastic seats and mops her forehead. A section of platform recently repaired with black pitch oozes under my feet.

'*Excusez-moi. Pouvez-vous m'aider?*'

A man is speaking to me. He is tall and thin and unshaven. I open my mouth to tell him that I do not speak French, when I feel another man grab the strap of my bag. He rips it from my shoulder with both hands. I turn my head and see the man with the bag running along the platform towards an exit staircase.

After an hour of searching, I see my bag sticking out of a litter bin three levels up, on the D platform for trains heading north to Orry-la-Ville. Inside is a paperback book, but everything else has vanished. Although they will be no use to the thieves, they have taken my documentation. My refugee papers are gone.

The top of my bag is smeared with a mouldy banana skin from the bin. The banana skin is mashed into the metal teeth of the zipper. I start to wipe it off, but it just makes more mess.

(None of this really happened.)

*

24th August 1990

'Alfred?'

Monsieur Bourguet is speaking to me.

'Alfred, that is what happened to your refugee papers, yes?'

I shake my head.

Passengers are reminded to keep their personal baggage with them at all times.

Monsieur Bourguet looks puzzled.

'I will tell you what happened,' I say. 'It was much worse.'

Diary extract
'A student came to my bench today. He said he had read an interview in the newspaper about my situation. He was from Bordeaux and was a student of business but had not completed course yet. He asked questions. I told him that I always pay for my own travel by myself. For twenty years I've travelled in Europe. The big European countries are very different *touristique*. I haven't travelled to the USA or Canada. I came from Belgique to Paris to London, then I returned to Paris from London airport. My end destination is not sure.'

Chapter 13

24th August 1990
I am sitting on my bench in Terminal One, Charles de Gaulle airport, on the departure level talking to my lawyer, Monsieur Bourguet. Some people say that, from a distance, Terminal One looks like a cross between a flying saucer and a doughnut. It is made of grey cement and has become very dirty on the outside because of all the exhaust fumes from many car, bus and aircraft engines. The lowest level of Terminal One is the boutique level, where there are the shops like

the newsagent, the dry-cleaner, a clothes shop, a CD shop, some restaurants and the Bye Bye Bar. On the next level, where the bus from outside drops passengers, are the airline counters. Each airline has its own counter, although some small companies use the counters of other larger airlines.

'Alfred, tell me what happened to your refugee papers?'

When passengers have checked in at the airline counter and given over their suitcase, they must receive their boarding pass. They can then go through one of the six preliminary boarding gates, which are escalators inside what the airport calls 'electric tubes'. These electric tubes criss-cross through the empty space at the centre of the building, carrying passengers over the fountain.

'Alfred, I don't want to talk about Terminal One.'

The electric tubes take passengers up to the third floor, where gates called satellites take them to the correct aircraft for their journey. On the next level up, on the fourth floor, is the arrival area, where passengers who have just landed have to go through customs.

'Alfred.'

Above the fourth floor are the offices of people who work at the airport, and on top of Terminal One, on the roof, is a car park, also for people who work at the airport and airport employees.

'Alfred, please tell me what happened. It's all right. Just tell me. Whatever it is. No more Terminal One. Just tell me.'

17th April 1986

I am standing on the bow of a ferry sailing out into the North Sea. I am forty-one years old and the sun is shining on my face. The boat is rocking with the waves that hit the stern.

I am going to England to find my origin. I have been through passport control leaving Belgium and I am now on an English ferry heading for England where I will become a British citizen. In my hand is an envelope. It is not sealed.

Through the North Sea mist I see an oil tanker slowly creeping into view, becoming larger and larger on the horizon like a building sailing through the water. At least, I think I remember the oil tanker. I am not sure when I saw the oil tanker, and when I remember things again this time there is no tanker.

I go downstairs into the bar and buy an espresso. I take it outside to where I can see the sea and sit at a table. I open my shoulder bag and take out my refugee card and my permit, stamped by the British Consulate, which allows me permission to visit England. At last they will not refuse my proposition to enter.

I do not need these any more, because I am through Belgium passport control and on an English ferry. I am already out of Belgium so I have no use for these documents any more.

I take envelope and write on it the address of the United Nations High Commissioner for Refugees in Brussels, Belgium. It is important to return documentation to its correct place. I put the documentation into the envelope and seal it up. The gum on the back of the seal tastes bad.

I drink my espresso watching the sea. It is grey and rough today. Soon I will be in England and I will discover my point of origin.

On level two of the ferry there is a post office. There is no queue. I buy the correct postage to Brussels and then stick the stamps on the envelope. The stamps have the Queen of England's head on them because I am now in England.

There is a voice on the announcement system giving passengers such as myself useful and relevant information. The voice says we will reach England in approximately fifty minutes.

By the entrance to the post office is a postbox. I put the envelope into the box, hold it half in and half out for just a second, and then push it inside.

Passengers are reminded to keep their personal baggage with them at all times.

I am in England and I will soon have revealed to me my point of origin. I am in England, and soon I will be British citizen.

24th August 1990

'My God, Alfred, so you posted your documents back to the United Nations High Commission for Refugees?' says Monsieur Bourguet.

'Yes.' I nod my head.

'What happened? They would not let you into United Kingdom without your papers, surely?'

'No, it was catastrophe. When I arrived in Dover, England, they asked for my documents. They refused me entry because I had no papers. I was kept in a transit zone inside the port and then they put me on a boat and returned me to Belgium. But Belgium refused me because I had no papers, and they put me on a ferry and sent me back to England.

'England refused me again, and put me back on a ferry and sent me to Belgium. Belgium refused again, and again put me on a ferry to England. That was the fifth time I crossed the North Sea on a ferry. When I reached England that time, they said that as I was refused in England and in Belgium, they would try France. So they sent me to France.'

'And did France refuse also?'

'No, France did not send me back to England. They allowed me to enter, but arrested me and put me before a court that found me guilty of entering France in illegal manner, even though I did not wish to come to France. Only the British authorities decided I should come to France. The court sentenced me to prison. That was the first time that I went to prison. I have been to prison three times now. I do not wish to go any more.'

Monsieur Bourguet shakes his head and says, 'Alfred, this should not have happened to you. Now I know you have previously been accepted as a refugee by the United Nations High Commission, we will appeal. The French judge cannot find you guilty again.'

It is difficult thing to talk about making such a mistake when it is you that has made the mistake. Sending my documents back was bad because I was not in England already. I was on a boat. It is difficult to think of such a big mistake. If you are in Charles de Gaulle airport, Terminal One, and you see me on my red bench from the Bye Bye Bar, please do not talk to me about such things because it is difficult and if you do then I will read a newspaper instead.

3rd September 1990
Monsieur Bourguet has written an appeal against the decision of the court. He gave me a copy of the document for my records which I keep in a bag. The bag has a small padlock that locks the zip, so the bag cannot be opened and the documents inside are safe.

This is some of what Monsieur Bourguet's appeal says:

<u>To the Presiding Judge and Advisers Making up the 11th Chamber of Paris Court of Appeal</u>

CONCLUSIONS

<u>FOR</u>   M. Mehran Karimi NASSERI
                 Known as 'Alfred MEHRAN'

APPELLANT

<u>Whose lawyer is</u>   Maître Christian BOURGUET,
                 16 Av. De l'Observatoire Paris
                 6ème. Tel: 46.33.33.55. Palais de
                 Justice B. 452

<u>AGAINST</u>   Le Ministère Public

CONFIDENTIAL

Ruling on the appeal properly lodged by Monsieur MEHRAN against a sentence passed by BOBIGNY County Court (17th Chamber), on 20th March 1990, which found him guilty of the charges brought against him, namely illegal entry to or residence in France, postponed the case to 26th September 1990 to rule on the penalty, ordering Monsieur MEHRAN to produce herewith a birth certificate and the supporting evidence for his approach to the OFFICE FRANCAIS de PROTECTION DES REFUGIES et APATRIDES.

(...)

Given, in fact, that the Court, in confirming that Monsieur MEHRAN was arguing for status as a stateless person, first of all ruled that it was his responsibility to establish that status, and that he could not be considered as such in the absence of recognition by a European Authority, given that the OFFICE FRANCAIS had not recognised such a status.

(...)

That Monsieur MEHRAN on these grounds maintained by way of objection that he could not be subjected to a penalty because his status as a refugee or a stateless person should have been recognised, the Court was obliged to rule on this objection and assess whether, in view of the facts of the case, it appeared that the accused satisfied the definition:

- Either of _refugee_, as defined by Article 1, A of the Geneva Convention of 29th July 1951.
- or of stateless person according to the regulations set out in Article 1 of the New York Convention of 28th September 1954.

Given, in fact, that if M. MEHRAN corresponded to one or other of these regulations, he could not, by the application of the regulations of each of these Conventions, be subject to a penalty because of his illegal entry to or illegal residence in France.

149

– I – ON STATUS AS A STATELESS PERSON:

That M. MEHRAN, having been on several occasions arrested and even convicted in France, his date and place of birth had already been checked and established by the French Police Services.

Given that, having been born in Iran, in a part of the territory of that country which, at the time of his birth, had been conceded to the Anglo-Iranian Oil Company, and which was administered by an English Governor, the Iranian nationality of M. MEHRAN, who was also born to an English mother, is not established.

Further that it remains the case that Great Britain has hitherto refused to recognise his British citizenship.

That within these conditions he corresponds perfectly to the definition of the stateless person as defined by the New York Convention.

– II – ON REFUGEE STATUS:

Given that the files show that Monsieur MEHRAN has not had an Iranian passport for at least 15 years.
That Islamic law, applicable in Iran, allows a sentence of death by stoning for people guilty of adultery, made him fear persecution both because of his origins and because of his denial of Islam and Iranian nationality, in the event of his returning to Iran.

<u>FOR THESE REASONS:</u>

– To confirm that Monsieur MEHRAN, having asserted before the Chief Justices that he could not be the object of unconstitutional penal sanctions because of his status as a refugee or a stateless person, it was the duty of the Chief Justices not to state without any further information that responsibility for proof of that status rested with him, but to look into the facts of the case to see whether or not he corresponded to the definition of refugee or stateless person.
– That the principle of the separation of powers forbade the Court from taking refuge behind non-recognition of that status by the OFPRA.
– To state in consequence that in any case Monsieur MEHRAN now establishes that he has been recognised as having refugee status by the Representative of the High Commission for Refugees in BRUSSELS.
– Establish that there is no information to suggest that he has lost that status.
– Say and judge in consequence that he cannot be the object of any penal sanction, and acquit him of all charges.
(...)

– III – ON ARTICLE 64 OF THE PENAL CODE:

Given that it has come to light in the course of proceedings that since 11th July, Monsieur MEHRAN, who cannot and in any case does not want to return to Iran, cannot find a country of refuge, and finds himself obstinately refused entry to British territory, where he wishes to go to have his citizenship of that country established.

That the file in fact contains proof of his attempts to leave

151

French territory and go precisely to England, while he has not been able to find any country of refuge.

That in these conditions, contrary to his wishes, and because he is unable to find anywhere else to go, that Monsieur MEHRAN has ended up remaining on French territory, a wish that he has in any case demonstrated in a particularly explicit manner by going to live in Terminal 1 of ROISSY CHARLES DE GAULLE AIRPORT.
(...)
To say and judge in consequence by application of Article 64 of the Penal Code that no penalty can be pronounced against him, and therefore to acquit him.
(...)

10 October 1990
The court gives its answer to Monsieur Bourguet's appeal. This is an extract from it.

PARIS COURT OF APPEAL

DECISION

Pronounced publicly on FRIDAY 12 OCTOBER by the 12th chamber, 2nd section D of this court
On appeal of a judgement by the BOBIGNY magistrates court – 17th chamber – 20th March 1990

PARTIES INVOLVED BEFORE THE COURT

1. MEHRAN Alfred Alias KARIMI NASSERI Mohran born 19th November 1943 in MASJED SOLEIMAN (IRAN), son of Abdulkarim and Simone . . . unemployed,

bachelor, no fixed abode, Iranian nationality

Previous convictions, accused, free, appearing assisted by Maître Christian BOURGUET, barrister-at-law, MD 18.02.1990 ML under CJ 2.03.1990 appealing

2. <u>LE MINISTERE PUBLIC</u>, not appealing
(...)
<u>APPEAL</u> to be lodged
– on 30th March 1990 by Maître BOURGUET, lawyer, in the name of the accused.

<u>PROCEEDINGS</u>:
At the public hearing on Friday 14th September 1990, Monsieur BINAZZI, interpreter, swore to make his contribution to justice according to his honour and his conscience.
(...)

<u>DECISION</u> delivered after hearing of all parties, and after deliberating in accordance with the law.

Considering that the accused, who claims to have been born Mohran KARIMI NASSERI, and who now wishes to be known as Alfred MEHRAN, acknowledges that he arrived in France from Belgium without a passport on 8th August 1988, that on 15th November 1988 he tried unsuccessfully to go to England where he claims his real mother lives, and that he has since that time been living within the building of Roissy airport, where he was arrested on 18th February 1990 with no documents confirming his identity and authorising his presence in France.
(...)

It is immaterial that his birthplace, MASJED SOLEIMAN, is situated in a part of Iranian territory that was, at the time of his birth, the object of a concession to the Anglo-Iranian Oil Company, and that it was under British administration. The International Court of Justice in The Hague has refused to admit that the consequence of this concession was to create a sovereign state, and that the British authorities have refused to recognise his British citizenship.

Considering that it is thus established that, according to state records, Mohran KARIMI NASSERI was born in Iran to Iranian parents; that it is even more unfounded for him to claim that he is not Iranian since he admits that he had been issued with an Iranian passport, and that he does not allege that the Iranian authorities have deprived him of his original nationality; that he has no cause to claim to be stateless.

(...)

That he pleads that he deliberately parted with the identity papers that he had at his disposal, most notably with the original of his refugee certificate, before embarking for England, convinced that he would be allowed into British territory and that he no longer required the abandoned documents; that he was therefore unable to resist any constraint outside his powers preventing him from leaving France for any other state, although he admits that Belgium cannot refuse to receive him, and does not allege that the Belgian authorities have forbidden him to return to Belgium;

(...)

FOR THESE REASONS and those not in conflict with the Chief Justices's ruling, THE COURT

Rejects the objections raised by Mohran KARIMI NASSERI, aka Alfred MEHRAN;

Declares Mohran KARIMI NASSERI guilty of illegal residence as a foreigner;

Condemns him to three years' prohibition of French territory.

Says that his expulsion must not be to Iran, and must only occur after a reasonable period.

Confirms that the prefectorial authority has granted a residence permit allowing Mohran KARIMI NASSERI the reasonable period to which he is entitled.

Sentences him to pay the Crown Court and the Court of Appeal the sum of 340.35 Francs, including postal charge and court charge.

So the French court has made an order that I should leave the country. Where do they expect me to go when no country will allow me to enter?

Diary extract
'10:20 a.m. Dr Bargain came to see me. Talk about politics. Newspapers say that United Nations Security Council in New York voted to impose sanctions on Serbia. Yesterday I say to Dr Bargain that I would like to keep diary record of my time here waiting in airport. Today he brought me a packet of paper. Big size – maybe 500 sheets. I have pen from newsagents and when he is gone to medical centre I write date (30th May 1992) on top of page and begin writing diary starting with conversation with Bargain . . . By the end of the afternoon I have written ten pages. I use both sides of paper so it will last longer.'

Chapter 14

23rd October 1990
It is getting colder in the airport at night. The lady from the CD shop gave me a blanket from her house because she said that she did not need it and it would keep me warm. Winter is the worst time to live at the airport when it is cold.

The last decision from the court said that I was to be expelled from France and banned from returning for three years. My lawyer, Monsieur Bourguet, has written another appeal. He says that result is illegal because the court did not provide a translator for me so I could understand what was happening.

This is what my appeal says:

Cour de Cassation
Chambers Civiles
Memoire Ampliatif

For: Monsieur Mehran Karimi NASSERI
(...)
<u>FIRST GROUND FOR REVIEW: Violation Of articles 407, 408 and 512 of the Penal Code, 594 of that Code, lack of legal basis</u>

<u>IN THAT</u> the contested judgement does not confirm that the interpreter appointed to assist the hearing of 14th September 1990 fulfilled his mission at the hearing of 12th October 1990, in the course of which proceedings were pursued and concluded and the judgement was pronounced;

<u>WHILE</u> the presence of an interpreter is called for whenever his assistance is required; that the very appointment of the interpreter on 14th September 1990 in itself established that the accused did not have sufficient knowledge of the French language to follow the proceedings that took place the following 12th October, the date on which judgement was pronounced, so that the absence of the interpreter at this second hearing fundamentally invalidates the proceedings and deprives the conviction of any legal foundation.
(...)

<u>SECOND GROUND FOR REVIEW: violation of articles 5,
6 and 19 of the regulation of 2nd November 1945, 28 and
31 of the Geneva Convention of 28th July 1951, 593 of the
Penal Code, lack of grounds and lack of legal basis:</u>

<u>IN THAT</u> the contested judgement sentenced Monsieur
MEHRAN to three years of French territorial prohibition
for illegal sojourn:

<u>WHILE ON THE ONE HAND</u> Monsieur MEHRAN was
justified in invoking his immunity to prosecution
provided for in Article 31-1 of the Geneva Convention for
refugees arriving directly on French territory from the
country where their life or freedom was threatened; that in
fact, having been granted refugee status by the
Commission for Human Rights in BRUSSELS, but having
had that status rejected by the authorities, and been
forbidden entry to other countries, the defendant, who has
never intended to settle permanently on the territory of a
third country and who, since his arrival in FRANCE, has
made no secret of the reasons for his entry into and sojourn
in the national territory, should be considered as having
entered French territory directly in the sense of the text
quoted above, and was therefore not liable to prosecution
for illegal residence.

<u>WHILE ON THE OTHER HAND</u>, under the terms of
Article 28 of the Geneva Convention of 28th July 1951,
Contracting States are obliged to issue refugees remaining
legally on their territory with travel documents designed
to enable them to travel outside that territory unless
pressing reasons of national security or public order
decree otherwise; that in his written testimony in support

of his appeal, the defendant demonstrated that he had been in possession of such documents issued by the Belgian authorities, but he was unable to request their re-issue because he had been expelled from that country; that for these reasons the contested judgement, which does not dispute that Monsieur MEHRAN presented all the conditions required in order to be issued with the documents which would authorise him to stay in FRANCE could not, since he constituted no threat to national security or public order by his presence on French soil, penalise him for illegal residence.

(...)

Monsieur MEHRAN is effectively obliged to remain in French territory, as he cannot return to BELGIUM to have the documents re-issued to him, even though he can claim to be legitimately entitled to them. It is, therefore, because he has been expelled in this entirely illegitimate manner as decided upon by the Belgian authorities, that Monsieur MEHRAN has been unable to present the French authorities with the documents that would allow him to circulate freely in our territory and escape any form of prosecution directed at him on the basis of Article 19 of the 1945 Act.

It follows that in fulfilling the conditions set out in Article 28 of the GENEVA Convention, Monsieur MEHRAN could not be subject to penalties unless the magistrate confirmed that his presence on French soil was a threat to national security or public order. As this is clearly not the case, and as such a threat is not even alleged, the decision forbidding him to reside in FRANCE for three years is not legally justified.

The verdict should be quashed

(...)

Monsieur Bourguet says that now we must wait for the court to hear his appeal and give its verdict. In the meantime, I stay in the airport to avoid danger of being arrested as illegal person.

31st December 1990

Yesterday was a very busy day in Terminal One. Many people are flying home or away to be with family. Today is much quieter. The shops on the boutique level have shut early. Dr Bargain comes to find me on the departure level and say 'Happy New Year'. I tell him 'Happy New Year' too. He says that I should get my documents next year, in 1991.

18th January 1991

Saddam Hussein is still refusing to move his army out of Kuwait and now the war has begun. Everyone at the airport is buying newspapers or watching the TV reports to find out what is happening. A television has appeared in the staff canteen and is on all the time.

I got new batteries for my radio so that I do not miss any news. It said on the radio that during the night the Allies launched an air attack on Baghdad and Kuwait, using over six hundred planes including American high-level B-52 bombers. The proposition to make Saddam withdraw from Kuwait is called 'Operation Desert Storm'. The targets of the bombs are airfields, military stations and power plants.

I speak to Dr Bargain. He thinks that the airport will have fewer passengers for a while. He says that people do not like to go on holiday when a war is occurring.

5th February 1991

I am sitting on my bench on the boutique level in Terminal One, Charles de Gaulle airport, working for the French secret service.

Next to me on the bench is a tape recorder with two big reels of tape. The wheels are spinning around. I am wearing a pair of headphones over my ears. The headphones are padded with black foam cushions, which are very comfortable on the side of my head.

My job is to listen to the tapes and then to tell secret service agents what is being said on the recordings.

I first began to work for the French secret service yesterday morning at 10:40 a.m. I was sitting on my red bench reading a newspaper when two men wearing suits asked if they could sit down next to me. I said, 'Yes.' I noticed straight away that they were not normal passengers because they did not have luggage. Normal passengers always have luggage.

The first man said that they were agents for the French secret service and that they knew of me through police and government sources. Then he asked me if I spoke Farsi. I said, 'No,' and they looked unhappy. Then the second man said that they wanted me to listen to tape recordings made from countries in the Gulf War and translate from Farsi into English.

I said that I did not speak Farsi, and that I would help them. I could see from their faces that they found this response confusing. Then the first man switched on a tape machine and I told him what the voices were saying.

The second man said that they had a special place in Paris, where we could go to listen to the tapes, and that they had a car that would take us there. I explained that I cannot leave Terminal One, Charles de Gaulle airport, because I do not have the correct documentation. The men said that this was not a problem, but I explained again that I cannot leave the airport. The men said the same thing several more times, but each time I explained that my proposition is that I cannot leave the airport in case of arrest.

The first man walked a little way off and made a call on his mobile phone, then he came back and said that we could stay in Terminal One. I made the suggestion that we go downstairs to the boutique level because it is more private than the departure level. This is a good thing if you are working for the secret service.

Yesterday I listened to tape recordings all day until 6.00 p.m. This morning, the two men returned with the same tape recorder but different tapes. The system is that the first man presses a button on the big tape recorder to make it start playing. I listen to the voices in my headphones, then the second man presses a button on a small tape recorder that he is holding and I tell him what the voices are saying.

We work for several hours. When my voice gets weak, the first man buys espresso coffees and we take break from work to drink them.

'How long have you been living in the airport?' asks the second man.

'Two or three years,' I say.

He looks surprised.

'But I will reach my destination soon,' I tell him. 'I am waiting for the French authorities to give me my documents, and then I will be gone.'

When my coffee is finished, the first man switches on the big tape recorder and we start to work again.

In the middle of the afternoon Dr Bargain appears. The first man sees Dr Bargain and stops him before he reaches the bench. Dr Bargain shows the first man his airport identification, which is a card in a plastic cover that hangs around his neck. The card has Dr Bargain's name and also a small photograph of him on which you can see that the hair from one of his nostrils is coming out more than the hair from the other nostril. I do not say anything about this because it would be impolite.

Dr Bargain looks quite worried. Then I see the first secret service man reach into his pocket and get out an object shaped like a wallet. He shows Dr Bargain his identification. I am the only person without any identification.

The second secret service man is still sitting next to me, but he is not looking at me; he is watching people walking by. He never looks at me.

Dr Bargain comes over. 'Alfred, is everything all right?'

'Yes.'

'You are OK?'

'Yes.'

'I will bring you those things that you wanted later. I will see you here later, OK?'

I do not know what Dr Bargain is making reference to. He does not have anything to give me. Unless he thinks secret service will make me disappear.

When Dr Bargain has gone, the first man presses button on the big tape recorder to make it start playing. I listen to the voices in my headphones, then the second man presses a button on a small tape recorder that he is holding and I tell him what the voices are saying.

This is the system for several days.

164

26th February 1991

Allied forces have taken back the country of Kuwait. Newspapers report a ground attack in the form of a multi-pronged offensive, which means they are attacking from many directions at same time. US and Arab tanks attack from the Saudi border and marines storm Kuwait City. In the west battlefield, Saddam's elite Republican Guards were attacked by combination of British Desert Rats, US Cavalry and French Foreign Legion. The biggest fleet of helicopters ever used in a war – 300 helicopters – airlifted 2,000 soldiers into Iraq. About fifteen hours after the attack started, Saddam Hussein ordered troops to withdraw. The war is over.

26th April 1991

It is warmer at night now. I am here in Terminal One, Charles de Gaulle airport, waiting, waiting and waiting for the court decision. The machine that makes the French fries in Burger King was broken again today. Very bad.

18th July 1991

I am standing in the criminal chamber of the Paris appeals court with Monsieur Bourguet to receive the ruling on my appeal.

The judge asks where I have been living since I was last in court.

I say, 'Terminal One, Charles de Gaulle airport.'

The judge looks very worried and says, 'But is it not dangerous to have an Iranian in the airport during the Gulf War?'

I say, 'There is no danger because I have been

working with French secret service.'

For reasons that I do not understand, many people in the court laugh when I say this.

When people stop laughing, the judge delivers his verdict. I have been waiting in the airport for nine months for this verdict, since last October. This is the judge's decision:

REPUBLIQUE FRANCAISE
AU NOM DU PEUPLE FRANCAIS

Given that, if the accused or the witness does not speak the French language sufficiently well, the judge engages the duties of an interpreter; that it must be confirmed that the interpreter has supplied his services each time they were required;
(...)
But given that while the judgement instances the appointment of an interpreter and his taking of an oath on the occasion of the first hearing, it makes no mention of his presence or his intervention on 12th October; that it is therefore not established that the interpreter assisted the accused for all the substantial proceedings of the debate.
(...)
For these reasons, without any need to examine the second proposed grounds for review,

QUASHES AND ANNULS the judgement of the Paris Court of Appeal, 12th chamber, of 12th October 1990, so that it be judged once more in accordance with the law.
(...)

Nine months of waiting in the airport for this.

2nd August 1991

It is very hot in the airport. I move around and keep in the shade. It is hot on the departure level and on the boutique level.

7th August 1991

Monsieur Bourguet has prepared a new defence and has submitted papers to the court authorities. He says that because I was given the status of a refugee by the United Nations High Commission for Refugees in Brussels, then France should also accept me as a refugee. Monsieur Bourguet says that to find me guilty of the charge they claim, the prosecutor will have to bring evidence that my status of refugee has changed. The charge of providing evidence is not up to us; the prosecutor must do this. Monsieur Bourguet has evidence that I am a refugee; they must prove the opposite.

Now I must stay in Terminal One and wait for new court date. Again.

Diary extract
'3:15 p.m. Journalist from Finnish newspaper asked me to write a list of all the people I have written to asking for advisement regarding my situation. I have presented my case through communications with Members of Parliament in London, to Royal government, Queen Mother, President Clinton, and former President Carter. I have asked them for help.'

Chapter 15

14th December 1991

I am standing in the washrooms at Terminal 2b (level 0) washing my hands. The facilities in Terminal One are closed for a week, for repairs, so I have to come here.

The sinks are small but clean. They have no plugs so they can never overflow. There are three soap dispensers with pink handwash inside; one is jammed, another is empty. Only one of them is working and this is the one I use.

I am waiting in Charles de Gaulle airport until I must return to the appeals court in Paris to see if they will grant me refugee status. The court has to hear my case again because last time there was no translator present, which is illegal if the defendant does not understand French.

A man taps me on the shoulder. I turn round and he punches me in the face. My head jerks backwards. His fist hits my cheekbone. A woman swings a punch at my head but misses and hits my shoulder. The man punches me again. Harder. My jaw snaps shut and I feel my tongue get caught between my teeth. The woman kicks me on the leg.

'Hey!'

A man has just walked in and is shouting at them to leave me alone. Another man is poking his head out of a cubicle; his trousers are hanging round his ankles. His face is full of fear. The man and woman hitting me look at each other and then run for the door.

'You OK?' says the man. 'Why did they do that?'

Two men in uniform are standing over me, watching me carefully. The side of my face hurts when I speak. One of the policemen is taking notes.

'Can you describe the attackers?'

I tell him I did not get a satisfactory look at them because they attacked me from behind and it all happened very quickly.

'But they were of Mediterranean type? Is that right?'

I nod. The movement makes the side of my face hurt.

'Maybe you should see a doctor before you catch your flight?' suggests one.

I tell him I have no flight. I can see Dr Bargain in the morning, at the medical centre in Terminal One.

'Do you work in the airport?'

170

I tell him, 'No.'

'Then why are you here?'

Passengers are reminded to keep their personal baggage with them at all times.

I explain my situation.

'How long have you been here? Three years, no?'

'More than three years,' I say.

'I think I read something about you,' says the other policeman. 'There was an article. In *L'Evénement*. Was that you? My wife read that.'

'And articles in other newspapers too,' I tell them.

'Hey, you're nearly famous,' says the first one.

'Nearly,' I say. I smile but it makes my face hurt more.

8th March 1991

I am standing in the appeals court waiting to hear what will happen to me. On my left side is Monsieur Bourguet who has written many defences of my situation. On my right side is the translator appointed by the court – Monsieur Morrison, whom I only met twenty minutes ago.

The prosecutor makes the statement that he does not intend to provide evidence that I am not a refugee, so I say to Monsieur Bourguet that he cannot because I *am* a refugee. But Monsieur Bourguet says it is not appropriate to make comments when the prosecutor is speaking and that I should be quiet.

The prosecutor says that he is not pursuing the case further and he is dropping all charges that I am an illegal person in France.

Monsieur Bourguet is very pleased. I still have no

official papers, but this decision means that I cannot be expelled from France.

Monsieur Bourguet says that he will write to the French Minister of the Interior asking him for a staying permit for me, and also a travel document, because I am now accepted as a refugee and can claim such things. He says that when the documents arrive at his office, he will bring them to Terminal One, Charles de Gaulle airport, and give them to me. This is good result for me.

16th May 1992

I am sitting on my bench on the departure level of Terminal One waiting for news of my legal status. Today is a Saturday. The busiest days in the airport are Monday, Thursday and Friday – particularly Friday mornings when there are always many, many passengers. The quietest day is Sunday. There are never as many flights as other days and so there are fewer people. Also the shops on the boutique level are closed so you cannot buy anything.

A group of American students are queuing up at their check-in desk for a flight to Chicago. There are thirty-one students, male and female, and four teachers (two male, two female). I watch them arrive from a coach outside and line up at the check-in desk, putting their cases on the conveyor belt and collecting their boarding passes. When the entire group has checked in, the teachers lead them to the preliminary boarding gate; they make a single file as they step into the electric tube that carries them over the fountain in the open centre of the terminal. I watch them until they disappear from sight as they reach the other end on the third floor.

Every day thousands of people pass through Terminal One, Charles de Gaulle airport, but I am always here waiting for my identity. Waiting for my documentation to arrive. It is 11:15 a.m. What is going on in the world outside Terminal One right now? What is happening in Paris? What is happening in London? I wonder which flight is taking off at this moment. Who is travelling on it? I write the date at the top of a new page and write down my thoughts in diary. I write for long time.

At 1:15 p.m. I go to Burger King to purchase an order of French fries. I do not really like French fries because they are not good food to eat every day, but there is nothing else I can buy.

1st July 1992

I go to the post office on the boutique level to see if they have any mail for me from my lawyer or from British authorities. They give me a letter addressed to: 'Mr Myrhan, (Man stuck at airport for 3 years), Terminal one, Charles de Gaule airport, France.'

I have received official letters at post office before, but never letter from private individual.

Inside the envelope is a postcard. One side of the postcard shows a photograph of two rows of men sitting looking at the camera. There are six men standing in the back row and five men sitting in the front row. The men are quite old and the ones sitting in the front are each holding a hat on their lap. One man in the front row has no hair at all.

On the other side of the postcard there is a message in black ink that says:

Dear Alfred: I've read your story in the newspaper and I thought you might like to receive a postcard from Spain. My name is Lucia and I'm 27. This photograph comes from an exhibition, and it's been taken in the south of Spain. I really don't know what else I could tell you, I don't know if you've ever been in Spain. I live in Madrid, the capital, and my life is nothing out of ordinary. I've seen your photo in the paper and you look very sad. I hope this postcard, and many others, will cheer you up a little bit. I promise I will send you another postcard very soon. Best wishes, and good luck.

L.

I have never been to Spain and I cannot tell what Spain is like from the postcard because it only shows two rows of old men looking at the camera.

24th August 1992

I walk back to my bench on the departure level after a trip to Burger King. When I reach it I find that Monsieur Bourguet is sitting down waiting for me.

'Lunch?' he says, pointing to the French fries.

'Yes.'

'How are things, Alfred?'

'Same as usual. Nothing changes.'

I eat my French fries.

'Do you have my documents?' I ask Monsieur Bourguet.

'No, Alfred.' He shakes his head.

Monsieur Bourguet reaches into his right-hand jacket pocket and takes out his pipe. This means

174

it will be a long story.

'I wrote to the French Minister of the Interior asking them would they please provide you with a permit to stay in France, and also a travel permit, now that the court has admitted you are an official refugee. This you know. I had a reply almost immediately, agreeing that you can have these documents. However, before they can be issued, you must present your refugee card – not a *photocopy* of the card, but the original. I cannot argue with them, Alfred, because this is normal; this is how it works.'

Monsieur Bourguet takes a long drag on his pipe. I eat French fries. A woman with a trolley walks by my bench; the wheels of her trolley make a squeaking noise.

'I know that your refugee card is at the United Nations High Commission for Refugees in Brussels where you sent it from the boat, yes?'

'I was mugged in the subway,' I say with a mouth full of French fries.

'All right, you were mugged. But the important fact is, that's where the original is, yes? So I wrote to Brussels asking them to send it to me. No answer. I wrote again. Still no answer, so then I phoned them. First they beat around the bush, but in the end they said, "We are sorry, but we cannot send the original of the refugee card to you, even if you can prove you are his lawyer and that you represent him. We cannot give the original of the refugee card to anyone but the refugee named on the card, and he must attend our office in person to collect it."'

I take a napkin and wipe oil from the French fries off my fingers.

'So I said to them, "But he has no travel visa from France so he cannot enter Belgium." They said, "We are sorry, but it is not our problem. We cannot send the original document to either you or to him. He must come here. Sorry."'

'I can't cross the border, I do not have any documents,' I say.

'I know, Alfred. For years and years I have been working with the French representative of the UNHCR, so I went there and explained the situation, and I showed them the documents containing the court's decision. I said, "Please help me. Call your colleagues in Brussels. Ask them to send the original to you in Paris because you are both representatives of the same High Commission. It should be simple. Then Alfred Mehran can come to your office in Paris." They told me, "Sorry, there is no connection between the different representatives of the HCR in different countries. We answer to New York; we don't work directly between Paris and Brussels."

'So then I wrote to the Ministry of the Interior for Belgium in Brussels saying, "Please give him authorization to enter Belgium temporarily, just to collect his refugee card and come back." I wrote seven times and each time I got the same answer back: no, no, no, no, no, no and no.'

There are no more French fries left.

'So what should I do?'

Monsieur Bourguet takes a handkerchief out of his pocket and dabs his forehead. It is very hot today.

'I don't know, Alfred. I will keep trying, of course. In the meantime, if any journalists come to speak to you, tell them your story. Ask them to phone Brussels and find out why you cannot get your card.'

French fries are not good to eat every day.

24th August 1992

8:30 p.m. Monsieur Bourguet has gone. The airport is always quiet on a Saturday night. One lone air stewardess walks through the deserted departure hall, her heels clicking on the tiles of the floor.

I sit on my bench and write the conversation with Monsieur Bourguet in my diary.

I cannot go across the border to Belgium because I do not have a travel permit from the French authorities. I cannot get a travel permit from the French authorities until I show them my original refugee certificate. I cannot get my original refugee certificate until I travel across the border to Belgium to get the original in person.

But I cannot go across the border to Belgium because I do not have a travel permit from the French authorities, and I cannot get a travel permit from French authorities until I show them my original refugee certificate, and I cannot get my original refugee certificate until I travel across the border to Belgium to get the original in person.

But I cannot go across the border to Belgium because I do not have a travel permit from the French authorities, and I cannot get a travel permit from French authorities until I show them my original refugee certificate, and I cannot get my original refugee certificate until I travel across the border to Belgium to get the original in person.

Diary extract
'10:45 p.m. There is a television in the staff canteen so everyone can watch the football. I watch too. I prefer Manchester United and Italian league. France won the World Cup semi-final tonight. Everyone happy. When match ended several people hugged me. I did not like it.'

Chapter 16

18th October 1994
This is still my situation. The Belgium authorities will not let me cross the border to get my documents, and they will not post them to my lawyer or to me because they say I have to go and collect them in person. But I cannot cross the border.

I have now been living in Terminal One, Charles de Gaulle airport, for six years. I have two shoulder bags and a plastic bag full of my newspapers about politics and economics. I can move around the terminal wherever I want, and sit in the restaurant or in the Bye Bye Bar.

I receive regular mail now. Most letters are from people who have read about my situation in a magazine. All the envelopes are addressed in many different ways.

Some examples of names and addresses on the letters which have arrived are:

Mr Merhan Karimi Nasseri, Boutique Level, Charles De Gaulle Airport

Mr Myrhan (man stuck at airport near the shops), Terminal One, Chares de Gaulle Airport

Alfred the Refugee c/o Charles de Gaulle Airport

Sir Alfred Merhane, near Burger King, Charles de Gaulle Airport

Sir Alfred alias Merhan Karini Nasseri, underground chamber, Airport Charles de Gaulle

Monsieur Sir Alfred, c/o Hamburger Shop

Today I received this letter from New York in America.

8th October 1994

Dear 'Alfred':

We read about you, and your struggle, in the *Wall Street Journal*. Enclosed is some French currency for you to use as you may wish.

Please acknowledge receipt by signing your autograph on the enclosed paper, and mailing it back to us in the envelope.

We were at Charles de Gaulle Airport one year

ago when we landed in Paris for a visit. We then went to London and we really enjoyed our stay. We know that one day you will succeed in your quest.

We wish you well. Take care.

Yours very truly,

Brian, George and Ann Luedke

And also this letter from Berlin in Germany.

Dear Mr Nasseri,

I read your sad history in a german newspaper and I send you a copy of it hoping it will reach you. Please let me know if I can do something for you. In 1968 I was in Iran and many people helped me, I was a refugee from East-Germany that time. Later I studied Iranian in Berlin. Last year I wrote a booklet about Iranians in Berlin. Though it is written in German I would like to send a copy to you because I think you would understand much of it.

I am German but my husband was Assyrian (ashuri), so my name is assyr. Please let me know if my letter comes to you. I am praying for you! Kind regards,

Gabriele Yonan

5th November 1994

6:45 p.m. I am walking to Burger King to buy some French fries when I pass a bench (not my bench) and see a wallet lying underneath it. I pick up the wallet.

It is made of brown leather – nice. Inside is a credit card and many French franc notes. I take the wallet to the airport Lost & Found department, which is located near staff lockers on the boutique level, and give it to man there. The name of the owner is on the inside so they can post it to him, but I cannot post it because I do not have an envelope.

Later, a man from Lost & Found comes to my table.

He says, 'Alfred, why did you hand that wallet in? There is money inside?'

I say, 'I am not thief. I do not take other people's money.'

The man tries to give me some money as a reward. He says it is from the owner of the wallet. But I tell him, 'I do not take money.'

Later, he comes back again, with a tray of food from Burger King. I say, 'Thank you,' because I will take food. I have already eaten today and it is late now. I put out my sleeping bag on the red bench and put the food behind the bench. I will eat it tomorrow.

30th May 1995

Today I went to the post office to collect my copy of *Time* magazine. I have now made a regular subscription to *Time* magazine, using the money earned from a recent job of translation. The airport police employed me to translate from Farsi, which I do not speak, to English, which I do speak, for which they paid me.

At the post office I also received this letter.

Dear Mr Nasseri:

I read in the newspaper the other day about your unfortunate situation. The truth is that at first I chuckled to myself about your problem, thinking that it was just another example of how foolish and messed up a bureaucracy can be sometimes. When I gave it further thought, however, it began to sink in how sad and hopeless you must feel, and I was very moved by your plight. I can't imagine a more frustrating situation than yours, to be stranded in an airport where you do not speak the language.

I wanted you to know that I have written to the French embassy here in Canada, urging their government to do something to help you, and to the British embassy, asking that they grant you a passport. I doubt that my lone letters will have much effect, but I hoped that it would boost your spirits to know that someone far away was concerned about you and your situation.

You have my best wishes,

David Broderick

3rd September 1995

11:30 p.m. I am sitting on my red bench in the middle of Terminal One, Charles de Gaulle airport, waiting. At 11:45, Dr Bargain comes across the terminal floor. He is rubbing his hands together and has a big smile.

'*Bonjour*, Alfred. Are you excited?'

'Not really.'

'But you should be excited. Tonight we are going on

a secret mission, nobody can know about it. Secret between you and me.'

I look round to make sure no-one is listening and Dr Bargain laughs.

'It's just a joke, Alfred. It's all right.'

'Yes.'

'Seriously, Alfred, tonight you're going to leave the airport for the first time in, what, since '92? What, three years?'

I say, 'Yes, three years.'

For months Dr Bargain has been asking me to go to different locations with him. In the summer he goes to live in a house in Brittany, which is another part of France. He has to live there in the summer because he owns a house there. Many times he has asked me to come to his house with his wife and family, but I have to explain that I cannot; I do not have the correct documentation and if I am asked by policeman for my papers then I will have to go to prison. Dr Bargain says this will not happen because he is a doctor, but Dr Bargain's medical qualifications are not a relevant fact.

'Tonight you are leaving the airport and I am going to drive you around Paris. All the famous buildings will be lit up, Alfred, imagine it.'

I say, 'Yes, nice.'

We lock my possessions in the medical centre and then take the elevator up to the top floor of the terminal, where there is a car park for people who work in the airport. The sky is clear and there are many stars, even with the glare of the airport lights. Not many planes take off late at night because people like to sleep without engine noise.

We get into Dr Bargain's car.

'Are you ready, Alfred?'

'Yes.'

Dr Bargain turns the key and the car makes a grating sound. He turns it again and it makes the same bad grating sound.

'Oh, Alfred, she's not working . . .'

Then he turns it again and engine makes the correct noise. Dr Bargain laughs.

'I'm just kidding, Alfred, I'm just fooling around.'

We drive to Paris. It takes maybe forty minutes. Dr Bargain says that Mrs Bargain made him drink a lot of coffee before our secret, midnight trip, so that he would not fall asleep while he is driving.

'But who would fall asleep on a secret, midnight mission, eh, Alfred?'

In Paris, Dr Bargain drives us past many famous buildings: the Eiffel Tower, Arc de Triomphe, Notre-Dame. While we are driving around, Dr Bargain keeps saying, 'Look at that, Alfred. Look at this, Alfred,' although I am already looking at the things that he is instructing me to look at.

When we drive past the Panthéon, Dr Bargain does not say, 'Alfred, look at that famous and beautiful building where the greatest Frenchmen who ever lived are enshrined.' Instead he says, 'Alfred, look at that bar along the street. You see that one with the big green sign? That bar specializes in selling bottled beers from all over the world. They have over five hundred different kinds of bottled beers in there. Can you even imagine such a thing? Five hundred.'

1:10 a.m. We drive back towards Terminal One, Charles de Gaulle airport.

Dr Bargain parks the car in the car park on the roof and we get out. It is quiet now. No planes fly this late. We walk to the edge of the roof and look out over the airport. There are twenty, maybe thirty aircraft scattered along the runways in lines of threes and fours, like birds feeding. The runway lights mark out lines that stretch far away into the darkness. Everything is still. Everything is waiting for the morning when planes will start to fly again.

'Alfred, do you know who Hergé is?'

'Yes. I know him. He invented character of Tintin in a comic book.'

'I used to read Tintin when I was a boy. I read an interview with Hergé once, long ago. He's dead now. But in the interview he said that one day he wanted the whole of the next Tintin book to take place in an airport. I remember because I was already working here. He said that an airport is so rich in human possibilities, a meeting point for different nationalities, the whole world on a reduced scale could be found at an airport. He thought anything could happen there: tragedies, jokes, exoticism, and adventure. He was right.'

Dr Bargain has worked in the airport from when it was opened thirty years ago. He will not leave unless one day they make him retire.

'The airport is a very magical place, Alfred. Whenever a new nurse or a new doctor or a new ambulance driver starts working at the medical centre, I take them up to the control tower. I take them when the airport is really busy; when there is an aircraft taking off every few moments. I take them up to the control tower and let them look round all three hundred and sixty degrees, and I say to them, "Look at this. This is our country. We are the chiefs. We are the medical chiefs of all this. We look after seven thousand airport workers and forty-eight million passengers every year. All this is ours." '

'What do they say?'

'Usually they say "Ohhh." And they think I am mad.'

Dr Bargain laughs. And I laugh too.

'Come on, Alfred, let's go and get your bags from the medical centre. Do you want to come and sleep on Mrs Bargain's sofa tonight?'

I shake my head. 'I cannot leave airport without documentation.'

Dr Bargain presses the button for the lift and we start waiting again.

Diary extract
'3:12 p.m. Journalist interviewed me at lunchtime. He said, "Alfred, I wish I was living free like you with no worries." I say, "There are many benches."'

Chapter 17

29th December 1995
The airport is quiet, with fewer planes flying between Christmas and New Year. The Bye Bye Bar is closed for redecoration this week because there are fewer people around. Everyone is home with their families.

Burger King restaurant has closed down. It does not sell food any more. You cannot buy any more French fries there. But builders have been working on new restaurant section on boutique level and it opened and there is new McDonald's restaurant there. This is very good because I prefer McDonald's French fries.

I decide to go to sleep early because there is nothing to do. Tomorrow there will be more people, and more the day after that. I slip into my sleeping bag; inside it I take off my trousers and get ready to go to sleep on my red bench. Sometimes it is difficult to sleep with all the lights on inside the terminal. The fountain in the middle of the garden stops pumping water so I know that it is exactly nine o'clock.

I am drifting off to sleep when there is the sound of loud voices coming down the stairwell.

'Happy Christmas!'

Two men and two women stagger in the direction of the restaurants. The men are each holding a bottle of champagne.

'Bollocks. They're all shut.'

The restaurants closed an hour ago. They turn around and spot me as they come past my bench.

'You all right, mate?'

'Yes.'

'You miss your plane?'

'No.'

'Poor bastard, missed his plane.'

One of the men concentrates hard on walking and steps forward.

'We've just been on Concorde. Bloody brilliant.'

He looks down at his own hand and is surprised to see it holding a bottle of champagne.

'And we got this for you, mate. Merry Christmas.'

He hands me the bottle.

'Come on, we've got to find the hotel. We can get a drink there.'

He heads away. One of the women stops to light a cigarette, and the other one hands me a very large envelope and smiles. Then she runs off.

'I hope you get your plane, mate,' the first man shouts from the stairs.

I open the envelope and inside is a Concorde calendar for 1996. On each page is a picture of Concorde in the air or taking off or landing. I spend an hour looking through the pictures.

11th May 1996

I go to the post office and collect a copy of *Time* magazine, which has picture of a clock on the cover and the words: 'Is Time an Illusion?' There are also two letters. One letter I understand. One letter I do not understand. This is the letter I understand.

2nd May 1996

Mr Alfred Mehran,

I live in Stavanger, on the western coast of Norway. Today I read about you and your difficult situation in our newspaper. How you have been waiting for eight years for a solution. You must have a very strong personality to endure this crazy situation. I wish there was anything I could do to help. I am:
Ragnhild Østbye
Stavanger
Norvége

This is the letter I do not understand. It is written in thick black handwriting that goes diagonally across the page. Writing diagonally across a page is not usual.

I CAN READ ABOUT YOU OVER A YEAR AGO NOW AND NOW AGAIN. EXCUSE PLEASE MY HANDWRITTEN MESSAGE AND THIS STUPID EUROTRASH ENGLISH. WHAT A STORY WITH YOU. I'M SURE YOU'LL WRITE A BOOK ABOUT

THESE STRANGE YEARS. BUT I WAS SURE YOU HAD GONE BY NOW. THERE WAS YOU ADDRESS IN NEWSPAPER AND HERE IS MY STORY AND SOME REASONS WHY I WRITE JUST FOR YOU.

I LIVED AT PAST IN SOVIET AREAS IN OCCUPIED SINCE WORLD WAR II ESTONIA (NEAR FINLAND AND SWEDEN) NOW WE'VE THE INDEPENDENT COUNTRY BUT IN SOVIET TIMES SECRET SERVICE SPECIAL STAFF FOR GOOD IDEA ROBBERS AND SELLING IDEAS TO THE WEST. NOW IN OUR AREA OLD HABITS ARE NOT DEAD. AND IN FINLAND AND SWEDEN ALL REFUGEES FROM OCCUPIED OUR COUNTRY WERE AUTOMATICALLY NO PRINTED PERSONS. SO IN MY COUNTRY I CAN LOSE MY PRODUCTION WORD BY WORD (WITH SILENCE AT FIRST).

PLEASE TRY TO CONTACT WITH THE GRUBER FILMS COMPANY IN LONDON. ONE MEMBER OF THEIR ROYAL FAMILY OWNS IT AND FOR HIM IT'S AN EASY CAKE TO BREAK THE WALLS OF SILENCE.

YOURS,

GEORGE FOAM

PS I'M SOON 40 AND WITH THREE KIDS AND WITH EMPTY POCKETS FROM SOVIET TIMES. THIS HIGH EMPLOYMENT AND TAXES COUNTRY IS NOT THE BEST PLACE TO BUY AN EXPENSIVE VEHICLE IF YOU SAID NO TO MARRIAGE WITH CITIZENSHIP (I CAN READ THIS). GOOD LUCK FOR BOTH OF US. I NEED FOR ENGLISH LANGUAGE AREAS A TRANSLATOR. CHEESE HOLES. THE DUKE. PREDICTION BOOK

(PREDICTS POPE). HOW CAN WE JUMP OVER OUR LANGUAGE WALLS? I THINK I HAVE THE KEY FOR THIS LOCK TOO.

I put the letter in my bag and lock it shut so it cannot get out.

1st March 1997

My lawyer comes today to tell me that Belgium has made an offer regarding my situation. Now they say that I can cross the border without a travel permit if but only if I agree to establish and live in Belgium. This is not acceptable. I have waited for five years to get my original refugee certificate, so I can get a travel permit. I do not wish to establish in Belgium.

Monsieur Bourguet tells me that he said to them, 'You oblige him to stay in the airport for five years and now you ask for a condition like that? He does not want to stay in a country who refuses him the right to enter just for a few hours to get one single document that he needs. Please, you cannot do this.'

But they make no other offer.

Today I tried new Chicken Fillet Burger for lunch, but it was not as good as Filet-o-fish.

31st August 1997

7:10 a.m. Francis wakes me up on his way to open up the newsagent's. He says to me, 'Princess Diana is dead.' I turn on my radio and search for an English news station. They say that Princess Diana's limousine crashed in an underpass in Paris. She was taken to hospital but she died. Many people buy newspapers today because they do not believe it can be true.

3rd July 1998

I go to the post office and receive a postcard from Dr Bargain. One side of the postcard is a picture of an ancient temple. On the other side is a message from Dr Bargain which says '*Bonjour* Alfred.' It does not say anything else, so what is his purpose in sending it?

I have begun to take extra straws from McDonald's when I buy my McMorning breakfast every day. I take them out of their paper wrappers and then slide the end of one straw inside the end of another straw. Using this technique, it is possible to make a long straw. I am also collecting the plastic tops from McDonald's sodas, which I then slide along the straws. I keep the collection of straws and soda tops safe behind my bench.

The small washroom with the shower was flooded today. Everything was very wet because a pipe burst in the night. I use a washroom on the departure level instead.

2nd August 1998

My copy of *Time* magazine has not arrived at the post office and nobody can explain a reason why. There was a letter. This is what it said.

Dear Mr Merhan,

I read your story in the *New National Enquirer*. I am currently being treated for a sudden and total loss of my hearing in both ears, at the famous Mayo Brothers Clinic in Rochester. I will only be at this Holiday Inn for a few weeks, so I will include my home address should you decide to write.

I was feeling very sorry for myself. Then I read about how you have been mistreated and forced to reside at the Gaulle Airport. Reading about how well you are handling everything, made me stronger inside too. I would like to communicate with you and help you out if I can with some stamps, coupons, whatever. I haven't been working because of my illness, but I could manage a few dollars to help you eat and get by take care, write if you care to and let me know what you need.

William D. Facchini
Chicago, Illinois

I do not write back because I do not like to take money from people I do not know.

21st June 1999
I am sitting on my red bench from the Bye Bye Bar in the middle of Charles de Gaulle airport, talking to my lawyer, Monsieur Bourguet.

'Alfred, I will tell you what has happened and why I am here. For seven years you have been waiting here in the airport because the Belgian authorities will not let you cross the border without a travel permit, and to get a travel permit you have to cross the border to Brussels to get the original of your refugee card.'

I nod while Monsieur Bourguet lights his pipe.

'My pipe was stolen,' I say.

'What?'

'My pipe. I had nice pipe. But it's gone. Somebody took it. Now I can't smoke my pipe any more.'

'Alfred, finally Belgium has got tired of all these news articles about you. I had a phone call from the Belgium ambassador. He rang me and he said, "I have news for you." I said, "Thank you, what is the news?" He said that he had received instructions that you will be given authorization to enter Belgium, and that all you have to do is go to the Belgium Embassy in Paris with your travel document.

'I said, "How? Where do you think he will get that document?"

'He said, "From the French authorities."

'I said, "Sir, do you forget that the French authorities will not give that document until he has the original of his refugee card? That is the whole reason he wants to go to Brussels." He did not understand anything, Alfred.'

'They won't let me go to Belgium,' I say to Monsieur Bourguet.

'But, Alfred, two days later he rang me back. The press pressure is too much for them. They don't want Belgium getting a bad name. He said that they have decided to send you the original of the refugee certificate. They will send it to you here.'

Monsieur Bourguet gives me a big smile.

'I will receive it here?'

'Yes, and do you know how you will receive it?'

'I can receive mail at the post office,' I tell him.

'Yes, I know. But they won't send it in the post; they are going to send it through the French police.'

Monsieur Bourguet laughs because he finds this is an amusing situation.

'The police who used to arrest you for having no

papers will come and deliver your papers. Finally, after seven years!'

'It is more than seven years since I have been here in Terminal One,' I say. 'Since '88.'

'That's true, but I meant that we have been waiting for this single piece of paper for seven years, yes? Seven years waiting for one small piece of paper that you can fold up and slip inside your pocket. Seven years just for that.'

I say, 'Yes.'

'You will be able to leave the airport by Christmas. Maybe sooner. I have rung the Ministry of the Interior and made an appointment at a prefecture for 2nd September. The police will deliver your original refugee card to you before that date and then we will go there and get your new documents – your staying visa for France, and your travel permit – your *Titre d'identite et de voyage.*'

Monsieur Bourguet leans back and takes a deep drag of his pipe. '*Now* you are excited, yes?'

I nod.

On the next bench along from us I see a man get up. As he walks away, I see that he has left an empty McDonald's soda cup behind. I will add that soda top to my collection.

Diary extract
'A photographer makes me stand outside by a wall so that he can see planes taking off in the distance behind me for a good photograph. The journalist asks me if I have hope. I say, "Yes, plenty of hope." Journalist says, "But you don't have regular home life for all this time from 1988 to 1994?" I say, "No, but my waiting time is nearly over. Soon I expect to leave."'

Chapter 18

11th August 1999
I am sitting on my red bench from the Bye Bye Bar in the middle of Charles de Gaulle airport, waiting for the sun to disappear.

'Are you ready for the darkness, Alfred?' shouts Francis, as he heads to the newsagent's at 7:20 a.m to open up the shop for customers. Francis has worked in the newsagent's on the boutique level for two years, but he does not care about news except for receiving football results. 'You will need your torch if you want to buy a newspaper today.'

This morning everyone in the airport is excited because there is going to be an eclipse of the sun.

The newspapers are full of diagrams explaining

how this will come about. An eclipse occurs when the moon comes in between the sun and the earth, blocking the light from the sun. The moon is much smaller than the sun, but it is also much nearer, so they will appear to be about the same size in the sky above Terminal One.

During a solar eclipse, the shadow that the moon casts when it moves in front of the sun is only just long enough to reach the earth, so the area where the eclipse is total (100 per cent) is not very wide compared with the whole planet.

But this will not be happening in Charles de Gaulle airport today because the newspapers say only 99.4 per cent of the sun will be covered up here, which is a partial eclipse. The area where it is 100 per cent is called the line of totality and that will pass north of Paris, through the city of Reims. People are travelling to see it because this kind of happening does not occur often.

10th June 1972

Already it hasn't rained for three months. Everything is dust. It is four in the afternoon and I am sitting inside the Sofre Khane Sonnati Sangalag teahouse in the grounds of the Park-e Shahr in Tehran, waiting for my uncle. It is too hot to sit outside even under the shade of the plane trees, and anyway I do not like the parrots that live in the trees. They are dirty and sometimes drop things.

At the table next to me, two men are locked in a game of chess. They have been playing for more than one hour. They are good, I do not think I could beat them. The teahouse manager watches to see their next move and then walks past to serve a table of four students the tea (*chay*) they have ordered. The tea is served to them boiling hot and black. When the manager has gone, one of the students turns an empty cup upside down on its saucer, a terrible insult to someone near him, but he is joking and the other students laugh. He quickly turns it the right way up before the manager sees and throws them out.

The walls of the teahouse are plain with no decoration and near the far wall water pipes, called *qalyans*, bubble away, filling the air with the warm smell of tobacco smoke.

I am watching the manager, waiting to catch his eye to order another coffee when I see my cousin, Golam, come into the teahouse. He looks worried and looks around quickly. He notices me and comes straight over.

'You must come,' he says simply. 'It's your father.'

11th August 1999
Too many workers in the airport wanted to travel north to where the eclipse is total. These people had to write their name on a piece of paper, and all these names were put in a hat (or other container – I don't know what they used) and then drawn out to see who could have the day off.

Francis is working today, but his friend, Philip, who is his boss, has taken the day off and travelled with his girlfriend to see the eclipse in the line of totality.

There are many instructions in the newspaper, saying how a person should not look at the sun directly because this will cause blindness. I have cut out one page of these instructions with my nail scissors and I have read them carefully because they apply to my situation: the situation of a man who does not wish to become blind.

14th June 1972

I am sitting in a car on my way home from the funeral of my father. The car bumps and jerks along the road, its wheels throwing up clouds of pale dust.

A motorcyclist suddenly cuts between our vehicle and the kerb, and his handlebar scrapes the side of the car door. Tehran traffic is getting worse.

I am sitting in the back of the car and sitting next to me is my uncle. We are the only members of the family in this car. The others are in different cars. We have not said much to each other on the journey or on the way back because there is not much to say.

We approach a roundabout. There is a knot of cars and buses trying to get through. Another motorcyclist darts up onto the pavement to avoid the jam and a group of pedestrians scatter like geese. One man shakes his fist at the motorcycle as it disappears. There are twelve million people living in Tehran and not one of them can drive properly.

Things have been difficult at home. My mother has been very upset. Almost too upset to make conversation with me. Yesterday when I came home I stopped by the front door. Inside the house my uncle was having a terrible argument with my mother. I do not know what the disagreement was about. I heard their raised voices and waited for a moment before entering, but when they did not stop shouting, I decided to go away instead.

When I stop staring out of the car window, I see that my uncle is looking straight at me. He looks sad, but he makes an effort to smile at me. All of a sudden, I am reminded of when I was a boy and we climbed the volcano together. Near the summit we saw a family of sheep lying on their side and I said they were sleeping, but then we smelled sulphur and my uncle said that the sheep were not sleeping but something else.

The driver of our car spots an armed traffic policeman on the pavement at the junction. He brings the car to a shuddering stop in front of a red traffic light that he was planning to ignore.

'Your father was proud of you,' says my uncle, nodding his head. 'When you graduated and we came to see you at the university, he was very proud.'

I don't know what to say back to him.

'He was very happy when you got your degree,' says my uncle.

I don't know what to say back to him.

'Yes, and my mother too,' I say eventually.

My uncle looks straight ahead at the driver.

'Yes, and your mother,' he says quietly.

11th August 1999

A long time ago, when people were frightened of eclipses, the Persians thought that the sun was disappearing because a great monster was trying to eat it. The Chinese believed the same thing.

Usually, this monster was thought to be a dragon, although many others believed that a giant toad was swallowing the sun. I do not understand why a toad would swallow the sun, because a toad is an amphibian that likes water; it does not like fire.

At the start of an eclipse, people would rush outside and bang drums and gongs to make a very loud noise to scare the monster away, trying to make it cough up the sun and bring the light back into the sky. Indians in Peru used to shoot burning arrows into the air, as high as they could manage, in an attempt to drive away the creature that was attacking the sun and keep it safe.

Today, people no longer take part in these activities during an eclipse because there are many complicated diagrams in newspapers explaining what is really happening at such a time.

Passengers are reminded to keep their personal baggage with them at all times.

I wonder if the planes will keep landing and taking off during the eclipse, or if the airport will stop completely when it is dark. Will they switch on the lights along the runway? I have asked Francis what will happen, but he replied that he just works in the newsagent and does not know about such things. So I must wait and see.

16th June 1972

I am standing in the main room of my home in Tehran. Sunlight filters inside through the white curtains. My uncle is sitting in an armchair, holding a cigarette between the fingers of his left hand. He taps his ash into a metal tray on the arm of the chair and exhales a cloud of grey smoke.

We have just buried my father, his brother, a few days ago, but my uncle looks very grim; his expression suggests that he expects something worse.

The last week has been unpleasant. My father is gone. I thought he had longer to live, but suddenly it was the end. Cancer. Since then there have been arguments behind closed doors. No-one will tell me why. This evening, my uncle took me to visit the countryside around Tehran and we walked together in the early evening sun. I like my uncle, but he has not taken me to the countryside since I was a child. When I asked him why we were doing so now, he said only that he wished to walk with me because it was a pretty evening.

I feel as if I am waiting for bad news in a doctor's surgery, and I would rather be upstairs in my room, finishing my reading.

After a few more minutes, my mother enters. She opens a window, then she comes over and looks at me from a distance as if she has never seen me before. As if I am a stranger in her house.

The nail on the index finger of my left hand is longer than the rest of my fingernails; I rub it over my lower lip so that I can feel how smooth it is.

'I have something to tell you,' says my mother.

I hope I have not upset her in some way I do not know about.

My mother looks at my uncle, but he does not meet her eyes. I look at him too, but he is gazing at the floor and will not meet my eyes either.

Then my mother looks at me and says something that is clearly not true.

'You are not my son.'

Diary extract
'It is good to sleep at the airport because you cannot sleep late. There is always something happening to wake you up.'

Chapter 19

11th August 1999
'Come on, it's started.'

The man in the pharmacist shop pulls the shutters down and puts a note on the door that announces that he will return in ten minutes. I see the woman from the dry-cleaner's walking towards the stairs, following him.

In the left-hand pocket of my trousers is a ticket that says that my brown jacket will be ready to collect on Friday. I move the ticket between my fingers, then take it out to check the date. It says Friday.

Behind where I am sitting, the big glass window looks out onto the fountain at the centre of Terminal One. I stand up and move near the window, then press my head against the glass to look up at the sky. Things are changing.

16th June 1972

I am standing in the main room of our home in Tehran. My mother is speaking to me. My uncle is sitting in an armchair, holding a cigarette between the fingers of his left hand.

Sometimes in this memory, my older brother is also there. He stays in the shadows at the darker end of the room, away from the windows. He shuffles about and shakes his head. Sometimes in this memory, I have no older brother.

'I have something to tell you. Your father was your father, but I am not your mother.'

In the event of a loss of cabin pressure oxygen masks will drop from the ceiling.

Uncle puts his cigarette to his lips and takes a drag. Please remain calm.

'Did you hear me?' says my mother.

Pull the oxygen mask down and place it over your face like so.

'I am not your mother.'

Passengers should fit their own masks before fitting the masks of any infants or children travelling with them. Passengers are reminded not to panic.

I do not understand. Why is she saying this? She has washed me, and fed me, and clothed me, for more than twenty-five years.

Finally I say, 'What do you mean?'

The woman who is my mother, but who is now saying she is not my mother, makes me sit down.

'Your real mother was a young British nurse who worked with your father in his surgery at the Anglo-Iranian Oil Company. They had something together that they should not have

208

had. You are the result of that. You are not my son.'

She asks me if I understand and I say no, but she carries on talking anyway.

'I did not know about their relationship until your father told me that this nurse was pregnant. He wanted her to be protected and he wanted to keep the child. You. You are their child. We hid the nurse while she was pregnant and then lied about who your mother was to protect your father. You know that people who are found guilty of adultery can be stoned to death.'

Article 102 of the Iranian Penal Code: When a stoning occurs, the men must be buried to their waist and the women to their breast.

Article 104 of the Iranian Penal Code: The stones used in the stoning should not be too big (as the convicted should not be immediately killed) or too small (so that the target will not be missed.)

Children born as a result of adultery are not stoned, because they are not responsible for their circumstance, but such children have no rights in Iranian society at all. No rights of inheritance, no right to function in society, no right to exist. They are nothing. I am nothing.

11th August 1999
I am looking through the window, straining to see the sky above the fountain, when a voice behind me says, 'Alfred.'

It is Laurent Chevallier. He is wearing his glasses, which is not usual, and has a big smile on his face. He must have made a delivery at the airport today.

'How are you? I don't have any sandwiches for you

209

because the wife is down in the south of France sunning herself. She's taken the monkeys down to stay with my parents.'

He calls his children 'monkeys'.

Laurent Chevallier runs a courier company called Transports Chopart, which is a company which collects various items from one location and takes the items to another location very quickly. He comes to the airport to make a delivery or a collection and sometimes he comes into the boutique level because his wife is English and he comes to the newsagents to buy English newspaper like *The Times*.

Sometimes, but not often, he brings me sandwiches of prawn or crab made by his wife. They are very nice. You cannot buy such things here in Terminal One. Once he showed me a photograph of his wife, she was holding a birthday cake, and on the cake the number 3 was written in icing, but the bottom of the number had gone wrong.

'Alfred, are you coming outside to watch the eclipse? It's nearly time,' says Laurent.

'I cannot go because I have no security for my bags,' I say.

'But there is nobody around . . . look. Everybody is outside.'

It is true. I haven't seen anyone else for twenty minutes. The boutique level is nearly deserted. Most of the shops are shut with little notices in their windows.

'No-one will touch your stuff,' says Laurent. 'Come on.'

16th June 1972

I am standing in the main room of a home in Tehran and people are telling me things that cannot be true. They are changing my point of origin.

My uncle flicks ash from his cigarette into the ashtray, and says, 'We kept everything very quiet. Another consequence could have been that the nurse might have been killed. No-one wanted that.'

The woman who is my mother but is not my mother looks at him as if she does not agree.

'It was a big risk,' he continues. 'Your mother . . . your real mother was hidden, and gave birth to you before she was sent back to Britain. We could not declare you to be born then, but we waited until your mother . . . your . . .'

He does not know what words to use.

'Your other mother . . .'

The woman who is my mother who is not my mother stares at him.

'. . . was pregnant with another child, and then it was recorded that she had two children at the same time. It is not unknown in situations such as this. You were declared five or six years after your real date of birth.'

Cabin crew return to your seats.

I do not know when I was born.

Fasten your seat belts.

I do not even know the name of my mother.

Please return all trays to their upright position and prepare for impact.

I have lived for twenty years as one person and now, in a few moments, I do not know who I am any more. I do not know this woman who is standing in front of me. It is obvious that she does not want to know me.

Now the woman who is my mother but is not my mother is telling me that I have no rights to my father's inheritance. None. My father was an educated man; he worked for the oil company all his life. We have properties, buildings, possessions; we are a rich family.

I will not let them make me into a no-one. They cannot take away my identity.

'I will look for a lawyer and lodge a claim,' I say.

My uncle puts out his cigarette stub and opens the packet for another. The woman who is my mother but not my mother moves forward and wags a finger in my direction.

'If you bring a case you will not win. There will be witnesses to say that your father did have something with a young nurse. I will have no problem in providing evidence that things were as I say and that you are not my son. You are sure to lose.'

The woman who is my mother but not my mother turns and walks out of the room. I never ever see her again.

11th August 1999

The sun is gone. It's like twilight now and some of the automatic lights inside the building are coming on. We walk across the floor of the departure hall and the automatic glass doors of gate 18 slide open. Laurent walks straight through them, but I stop at the boundary of the building. Outside, everything looks grey.

There are many people on the pavement. I count

212

twenty-three members in a group of Japanese tourists. They are surrounded by suitcases and trolleys, and they are all standing staring at the sky.

Across the road, by the bus shelter where the airport buses pick up passengers to take them to the RER station and the other terminals, a man has set up a telescope. It is projecting an image of the sun onto a piece of white card. I have seen this method described in a newspaper as a safe way of watching the sun which will not make you go blind.

Laurent looks back and sees that I have stopped following him. He beckons to me. 'Alfred, come on. You can't see anything properly from there.'

I hold onto the edge of the door and lean forward, but I cannot see the sun from the doorway.

The nail on the index finger of my left hand is longer than the rest of my fingernails; I rub it over my lower lip so that I can feel how smooth it is. I move it back and forth to make sure that it is smooth all over.

Then I step outside the Terminal One building and walk over to where Laurent is standing near the man with the telescope. Even though the image is clear where the telescope projects it onto the card, I cannot stop looking up at the sky itself. I understand why people felt like banging a drum to bring the sun back and save it from a terrible monster.

16th June 1972

I am standing in the main room of someone else's home in Tehran and I do not know who I am any more. I watch my uncle light another cigarette. He tells me to sit next to him.

213

The woman who is not my mother but was pretending to be my mother has left. I never see her again. I do not know where my real mother might be or even what her name is.

My uncle says that this is a difficult situation for everybody and that it makes him very sad.

'You like England, don't you? I've seen your newspapers and your magazines. You're always reading in the university library and in your room.'

He looks towards the doorway to make sure the woman who is not my mother but was pretending to be my mother has gone.

'You could bring a case, of course, but you will lose. You cannot win because there will be too many witnesses. Probably no lawyer would even take the case on because you would be sure to lose.'

He offers me a cigarette and I take it. And he lights it for me with his silver lighter that my father gave him for his birthday five years ago. He waits while I take a drag. The live end of the cigarette sizzles and glows orange when I inhale.

'This is the deal. Three years in England attending an English university. All your studies, all your living costs, all that will be paid for. And after that, you go where you want to, but you don't return to here. Ever.'

11th August 1999

Everything is quiet now. There are no aircraft moving. There are no cars driving. Outside the terminal, the bus drivers have alighted from their vehicles so they can watch the sky. It is getting colder. I can feel the temperature dropping very quickly. A wind blows up from nowhere.

The sky slips from twilight into darkness. In a few moments everything in the world has changed.

Diary extract

'11:30 a.m. Last night while I was sleeping one of the shops on the boutique level had a break-in. I did not know of it until I saw many policemen this morning. One policeman came over and asked me if I heard anything but I did not hear anything because I was asleep. Policeman said that someone forced the lock on the front door, but did not set off the alarm inside.

The thief took many watches and jewellery. When I looked inside I saw the police putting white dust on the counter to try and find the robber's fingerprints.

It is easy to escape from a robbery at an airport because afterwards you can fly anywhere in the world and no-one would find you but you would have to steal only small things because excess baggage is very expensive.'

Chapter 20

2nd September 1999
I am sitting on my red bench from the Bye Bye Bar in the middle of Charles de Gaulle airport, waiting to leave. I have been here for eleven years. At ten o'clock my lawyer, Monsieur Bourguet, and Dr Bargain arrive

to collect me because three months ago he made an appointment for us to go to the prefecture.

'Are you ready, Alfred? You feel OK?' asks Dr Bargain.

I tell him I am fine.

'Today is exciting, yes?'

I tell him, I don't know.

'Because today finally we are going to the prefecture and you will get your documents.'

'Your *Titre de Voyage*,' says my lawyer.

'We can collect your documents,' continues Dr Bargain, 'and then you can leave the airport. You can go where you like. You will be free. You can legally stay in France. I heard an interview with you on the radio this morning, Alfred. I was eating breakfast with my wife and we heard you. My son said, "Daddy, that's Sir Alfred!" Everyone is waiting for you to have your documents. There were journalists here yesterday, yes?'

'Yes.'

'Are they coming back to see you finally leave the airport and get a plane out of here?'

'I don't know.' I shrug.

Before I can go I have to move all of my bags and possessions because I cannot leave them unsecured in a public area. Dr Bargain and a man from the reception at the medical centre help me move everything inside the medical centre so nothing will happen to them while I am away.

'They will take care of them. Come on, Alfred, let's go.'

We walk to lift twenty and go up to the tenth floor and out to the car park on the roof of the terminal building where Dr Bargain's car is waiting. An aircraft takes off and flies over our heads with its engines on full throttle. I see Dr Bargain watching me. He grins.

Dr Bargain and Monsieur Bourguet sit in the front of the car and I sit in the back. Dr Bargain drives for one hour.

The building we arrive at is small and is painted white and has a line of neatly kept trees outside. The air smells different than at the airport.

Inside the prefecture, a woman is waiting for us in the reception. Dr Bargain is still smiling.

'*Bonjour, Madame,*' says Monsieur Bourguet.

Everyone shakes hands.

'Alfred, this is Madame Tardi. She has your documents.'

Monsieur Bourguet says everything is ready. He reaches in his pocket for a his cheque book and writes a cheque to pay for the legal stamps that must go on the documents, then Madame Tardi hands a piece of folded green cardboard back to my lawyer. He reads it carefully and nods.

'*Très bien.*'

He hands it to me.

On the cover it says '*TITRE de VOYAGE AL No: 010445*'. Inside is a small passport photograph of me that was taken in the photo booth at Terminal One. It is a good photo except there is a dark shadow on my neck. Monsieur Bourguet says that doesn't matter and hands me a pen.

'Now all you have to do is sign here,' says Madame Tardi.

I read the card very carefully.

'I cannot sign it.'

'Why not?'

'I cannot sign it because it says I am Iranian.'

7th August 1975

I am sitting on the floor in a bare room and in my mind I remember a newspaper that I once read in the library of my university in England:

'Interrogation and torture methods in Savak prisons include, but are not limited to: electric shocks, whippings, beatings, inserting broken glass into a person's body, the forced extraction of teeth, the forced extraction of fingernails, the forced extraction of toenails, tying weights to the testicles, and pouring boiling water into the rectum.'

I remember this because it was in a newspaper in the university library and I copied out the paragraph into my page-a-day Letts diary. I do not have it now because the diary is in my luggage, and my luggage has been taken by the Savak.

There are sounds outside in the corridor and the two men watching me look towards the metal door of the room. It opens and in walks a Savak officer with papers under his arm. Two more men follow in behind him; they are carrying a small wooden table and two chairs. The two men set out the table and chairs and then leave. The officer sits on one chair, puts his files on the table, and then points to me and to the other empty chair.

I stand up. My leg is stiff from sitting on the floor. I sit opposite him, I do not lean on the table. The two men in uniform who have been watching me for an hour stand behind me in the shadows in the corner.

'Do you know why you are here?' asks the officer.

2nd September 1999

'So you are not Iranian?' says Dr Bargain.

'No.'

'But it's written on your refugee card.'

'I was Iranian, but I am not Iranian any more.'

Monsieur Bourguet sits down next to me.

'I am your lawyer. Do you trust me?'

'Yes.'

'This is how things work. When you are born in a country, then you have the nationality of that country until you get another one, which you have not done. You are Iranian as long as you are not of another nationality. If you sign these documents, then France has to accept you as a citizen, because of all the time you've already been in France, at the airport. There's nothing to be afraid of. You can sign.'

'There is another reason that I cannot sign. The name on this document is written as "Mehran Karimi Nasseri". I am not Karimi Nasseri any more.'

'So who are you?' asks my lawyer.

'Sir Alfred Mehran.'

Dr Bargain has stopped smiling.

We apologize to all passengers who are experiencing delays in the departure times of their flights.

Monsieur Bourguet tells me that the name on these new documents has to be the same name as the name on my old refugee card. He says that there is no way around that.

'When I arrived at the airport I was Mehran Karimi Nasseri, but I have been waiting there eleven years. I have changed and I am not the same person today as the person who first slept on the airport bench eleven years ago. Now I am Sir Alfred Mehran. My

221

documents must say this. How can I accept it otherwise?'

They ask me to sign them several more times, but I cannot. The documents do not have my name on them, so signing them would make a forgery. Monsieur Bourguet and Dr Bargain whisper to each other and then I go outside with Dr Bargain to wait by the car. Dr Bargain does not say anything. My lawyer stays inside for a few minutes talking with the woman, then he comes out and says, 'There's a *tabac* over the road – let's get a coffee.'

I order an espresso, and while we wait for our drinks to arrive my lawyer and my doctor talk about things.

'This is a difficult situation, Alfred. The lady in the prefecture is trying to be helpful, but they have to put on the form the name that was on your other papers. They can't change it.'

'Yes, I understand.'

'So, will you sign it?'

'No, I cannot sign it.'

Monsieur Bourguet reaches inside his jacket and pulls out the *Titre de Voyage*.

'Alfred, I persuaded the woman to give me this for you. Usually it has to be signed in front of an official, but for you she made an exception because you are special. Keep it safe and sign it when you want to.'

'I cannot sign it because it says that I am from Iran.'

'I know, but keep it anyway. You might decide you want it in the future and where is the harm in keeping it?'

He hands me the *Titre de Voyage* and I put it in my bag.

'We have been trying to get you those documents for nine, no, ten years,' says my lawyer, taking out his pipe and flicking a flame from his silver lighter.

I nod. He lights his pipe and inhales.

'In all that time I have not received one single franc. I appeared before three different courts for you, all that for free, for nothing. And now that we're here, you have documents in your hands that will allow you to go free. If you sign them, you can go where you want.'

There are many places I don't want to go, like Belgium. Not nice.

Dr Bargain puts his coffee cup down and it bangs on the saucer. Some liquid flicks up and spills on his fingers. He takes out his handkerchief to dry himself.

I hope my possessions in the medical centre on the basement level of Terminal One are safe. I do not like to leave them in an unsecured area.

'Why don't you sign the documents, Alfred? You can be free.'

'I am not Iranian.'

'OK, you say you're not Iranian any more, but you were born in Iran, right?' asks my lawyer, putting his pipe to his mouth again.

'No,' I say.

'If you were not born in Iran, then where were you born?'

I tell my lawyer and Dr Bargain where I think my point of origin might be. Neither of them speaks for several seconds. I drink my espresso. My cup has a very thin rim that feels sharp against the end of my tongue.

'So you are saying that you were born in Sweden?'
I nod.

24th August 1951

I am standing in a hall. It is late afternoon and it is very hot. There is no breeze coming in the open windows, only more heat. Inside, walls that were painted white long ago are now covered in dirt, dust and fingermarks. I am acting with a group of boys who are older than me, much older. They are young men. I am not acting myself; I am only five years old. I am the prompter, and when people forget their lines I remind them what they have to say.

The students are rehearsing a play. In a few days they are going to perform the play in the town square to an audience. They are not very ready.

The play tells the story of Nader Shah, who was the Shah of Iran from 1736 to 1747. He was the last of the great Asian conquerors. He won many victories, but in the end he became a tyrant who feared the theft of his throne so much that he had his own sons blinded so that they would not be a threat to him. His rule came to an end when officers from his own guard could not stand to watch any more injustice and assassinated him.

It is said that one of his most successful campaigns was into India during which he recovered many treasures, including the Kuh-e Nur diamond and the Peacock Throne – a throne encrusted with 26,733 precious stones and gems.

In one corner of the hall is a threadbare old armchair that is falling apart and I think may have small things living inside it. This is our Peacock Throne.

One of the players stumbles over his line and gets the words wrong. I tell him what they should be. In my memory I am five years old.

We have been rehearsing all day and I am tired and thirsty and someone else makes a mistake and I correct them, only this time it is me that is wrong.

'I know my part. I know who I am supposed to be,' says the student.

He comes over with two of the other actors. They are taller than me. They take hold of my arms, move me across the room and sit me in the armchair. Then they go back to performing the scene as if I am playing the Shah watching them from my dusty armchair throne.

I watch them carefully. If someone makes a mistake, I am not sure if I will correct him or not. One of the conspirators unsheaths a long dagger ready to stab the Shah. In a play, a dagger should be springloaded with a special contraction. So then, when someone is stabbed with it, the blade collapses and they only look as if they are being stabbed.

This dagger is not springloaded. When they stab me to assassinate the Shah, I feel the sharp point break my skin and penetrate my body. There is blood on my white shirt.

They take me to hospital where I cry, while the doctor does something with a needle and thread. I still have the scar.

2nd September 1999

'You think your point of origin is in Sweden, but your earliest memory is being a prompter in rehearsals for a play, in Iran, when you were five,' says Monsieur Bourguet slowly.

'Yes.'

'So how did you get from Sweden to Iran?'

I tell him and then there is silence for a minute.

The nail on the index finger of my left hand is longer than the rest of my fingernails and I move it over the lower lip of my mouth so that I can feel how smooth it is.

Nobody speaks while we drink our coffee, although my lawyer, Dr Bargain and I have no more coffee left. I lift my empty cup anyway. I touch it against my tongue again.

'And what makes you think that?' says my lawyer finally.

'Because I remember it was closed in,' I say.

'And so you're sure that when you were a small child you were taken from Sweden, where you might have been born, to Iran, underwater in a submarine.'

I nod. 'Yes. I am certain. How else would I get there?'

No-one says anything for a while, then I follow Monsieur Bourguet and Dr Bargain back to Dr Bargain's car and we drive back towards the airport.

'If you sign those documents, Alfred, they will let you stay in France, yes?' says Monsieur Bourguet. 'Then everything will be all right. Will you think about it?'

'Yes.'

'Good.'

226

'But I cannot sign them because I am not from Iran.'

On the way back, Dr Bargain drives a little too quickly I think. Dr Bargain parks his car in the car park on the roof. Only special people and airport employees are allowed in this car park for security reasons. We say goodbye to Monsieur Bourguet, and then Dr Bargain and I go down to the basement level in lift twenty.

'Relax, everything is safe, Alfred,' says Dr Bargain. 'Your belongings are all in the medical centre, remember?'

'Someone might take them.'

'Are you worried that a doctor will steal your collection of McDonald soda tops?'

I tell him that I do not think a doctor will steal the long straws and soda tops. 'But, maybe radio, or clock,' I say.

Dr Bargain smiles for the first time in an hour.

My possessions are still inside the room and everything seems satisfactory. Radio, clock, everything is there. Dr Bargain and a driver of the airport ambulance help me move my things.

When we get back to my bench, someone is sitting on it. I do not know who they are. I have to shoo them away by waving my hand. They look puzzled but they leave. They shouldn't sit in my special place on the bench that belongs to me.

I lay out my sleeping bag on the red bench and begin putting my things where they belong. Clock, and radio, and paper behind the red bench. My bag of newspapers goes on the left-hand side, acting as a barrier to make things more private. The trolley with the five grey Lufthansa boxes also goes on the left-hand side. I hang my clothes (in plastic from the dry-cleaner's) on the back of the red bench from the Bye Bye Bar. The long straws with the soda tops on them go behind the bench where they are safe.

Dr Bargain sits down on the black chair at the table in front of my red bench.

'Alfred, you have your papers now. When you are ready, you can sign them, and then you can leave here and you can go home.'

Passengers are reminded to keep their personal baggage with them at all times.

'Do you understand?'

I nod, but really it is Dr Bargain who does not understand that I am already home.

Diary extract
'7:50 a.m. When I return from men's washroom from shaving, there is a plate on my table with one piece of apricot tart and one piece of chocolate torte from café owner. Chocolate torte – good. Apricot tart – dry.'

Chapter 21

23rd September 2000
I am sitting on my red bench from the Bye Bye Bar in the middle of Charles de Gaulle airport waiting for the director to say 'Action'.

Around my bench are seven members of the film crew holding lights and sound equipment. The airport has given special permission for us to make a film on its property. The film is about my situation, which is the situation of a man who has been living on a bench at an international airport for twelve years because he does not have the correct documentation.

The film is going to be called *Here to Where* and the man who is directing it is called Glen Luchford, who is from England although sometimes he lives in New York. He visited me with Paul Berczeller in the summer, to discuss making such a film. They came to my bench on the day that the Concorde crashed.

I am happy to make film because it will draw attention to my situation and make a better impression for me in the airport. People will see that I am earning money from the film which will improve my image.

Glen is a fashion photographer and his pictures have been in many magazines like *Rolling Stone*, *Vanity Fair* and *Vogue*. I do not read these types of magazine because I prefer political publications, such as *The Economist* and *Time* magazine. I asked Glen if he had made photographs in *The Economist* but he told me 'No'.

Before we started filming, Glen told me that when his aunt left his uncle, his uncle stayed inside his house for many years. He said it is probably because of this that he is drawn to the idea of self-imprisonment. I said that this is irrelevant to my situation because I am not someone's aunt who has left her husband, and I am not living in a house. I am living in an international airport because I do not have the correct documentation. Glen said, 'Yes.'

Glen says that the following writing will appear on screen at the beginning of the film. The writing will say:

'On 15th November 1988, Alfred Mehran, a stateless refugee from Iran, landed at Charles de Gaulle airport. Refused entry by France and every other country, with nowhere else to go, he waited on a bench in the basement of Terminal One, while lawyers tried to rescue him from bureaucratic limbo. It took them eleven years to win Alfred his freedom. But the airport had become his home. To this day, he remains on his bench – waiting.'

I do not know why it says that I am from Iran because my point of origin has not yet been decided. I am waiting for my documentation on that subject.

In most of my scenes I am acting with Paul Berczeller, who is an American. Paul is an actor, but in the film Paul is pretending that he is the director of the film and that things are not going well for him. Glen says that the film will be a 'mockumentary', which he says is like a pretend documentary with comedy. I am not doing comedy. I am acting as myself. I do not have to learn a script, but just make conversation with people. But the days are long and I am quite tired by the end. Last night, when Glen was talking to me, I nearly fell asleep in front of him, which is not good.

I am happy to be in the film, but I have told Glen that I would like some new clothes to wear. I have no new clothes because it is not easy to buy such things in Terminal One.

Also I have lump on my head. Infection. It is a lump about 3cm tall, halfway back on the right-hand side of my head. It is caused by drinking too much coffee, especially strong espresso, and is also caused by fake cola products. The lump does not look good so it is important that I have new clothes to appear in the film, and that I am clean-shaven, so I can give a good impression. Glen has asked me not to pick at the lump on my head while we are filming scenes.

29th September 2000

I am sitting at a table opposite Paul in the restaurant area. We are eating lunch and a crew is filming our conversation. I am eating French fries from McDonald's, which I prefer to French fries from Burger King.

231

'I'm very happy you're going to be in my film.'

I have to think of something to say back to Paul, so I say, 'Thank you very much,' and then I wipe my nose with a napkin. I do not wipe my nose because I am acting, but because I need to wipe my nose.

Then Paul says, 'I'm sure you're going to be a very good actor and you understand exactly what it is I want to do, right?'

I say, 'Yes.'

'I want you to play yourself. I don't want you to play another role. I want you to be yourself. And then I have to find some other actors for you to act with. You wouldn't mind working with Iranian actors, would you?'

I eat another French fry.

I tell Paul, 'I don't know them.'

'No, but you wouldn't mind that would you?'

I tell him again, 'I don't know them.'

I ask him when the film will be shown on the screen.

'If everything goes OK,' he says, 'it will be in the film festival next spring.'

Paul leans forward and smiles. 'If our film goes to the Cannes festival, would you come there with me?'

'If I have my regular documents from the authorities,' I say, 'then I would do a much better job of representing the film at the Cannes festival.'

Paul is smiling and getting excited.

'Imagine you and me in tuxedos going down to the South of France – yachts, girls in bikinis. We'd go, and they would show our film in the festival. And then afterwards, when it was over, we'd walk down the aisle, along the red carpet, and stand on the stage, and

232

everyone would be applauding us. Wouldn't that be great?'

Paul has a very big imagination.

'Just like hoping my toes recover before next spring. And I can walk smoothly,' I say, because I have trouble with my feet.

Paul smiles. 'We'll have to work on your toes, Alfred.'

'I think there is no reason why they delay the solution to my document problem.'

I take drink of cola through my straw. When we have acted this scene, I will save the top from my soda.

'Alfred, I would love to see you on the stage and everyone applauding because you had left the airport. And because we had made this movie together. Imagine how great that would be. It would be amazing, Alfred. Amazing.'

I eat French fries until Glen says, 'Cut.'

3rd October 2000

Paul and Glen asked me if there was anything that I would like to see on film from the outside world, because they have special camera which runs on batteries and they can film things and then play it back for me at my table. I said that I would like to see the site of the Concorde crash.

On 25th July 2000, a catastrophe occurred as an Air France Concorde took off from Charles de Gaulle airport, heading for New York. The flight number was AF4590 and the aircraft was carrying many German people. As the Concorde reached an altitude of approximately seventy metres, witnesses saw fire coming from one of the engines on the left side. The Concorde aircraft rolled over onto its left side and then crashed into the Hotelissimo hotel in the town of Gonesse. One hundred and nine people on the plane were killed, and four people on the ground, giving a total of one hundred and thirteen fatalities.

Paul and Glen took a camera to the crash scene, which was beside a road and sealed off behind fences. They made a video film of the area and then played it for me at my table. There used to be a hotel at that location but Concorde crashed onto the hotel and it is not there any more.

I asked Paul if he would put it in the film and he said, 'Maybe.'

17th November 2000
I am standing in front of a sink in the washroom. I have foam on my face because I am shaving. Paul is at the next sink; he is wearing a white T-shirt and jeans and he is also shaving. Paul is shaving with a razor made from blue plastic, but my razor is made from white plastic. Three months ago I lost a razor. I never found it again or discovered what happened to it.

The washroom walls are covered in small blue-grey tiles that make it look like a public swimming bath. By the doorway is a notice about what is allowed to happen in the washroom, and what is not allowed to happen in the washroom. Although this notice applies to me, I did not read it when I walked in because I have read it many times before.

'I'm worried because I'm not going to be here as much,' says Paul. 'And I'm worried about what's going to happen with you.'

He does not need to worry. I am waiting for my documents.

'I followed my identification,' I say, and then I wipe foam from my left cheek.

'But you've been doing that a long time, right?'

'Yes. It takes longer,' I say.

'I know, but nothing has changed, Alfred.'

I tell him many things have changed.

'What's changed?'

'My documents, my papers.'

'But you're still here, Alfred, right? You're still at the airport.'

'Yes. One of the airport's passengers. I'm always a passenger. If I go, I come back again. I've been outside several times and always I've returned.'

'I know, but you haven't left in years now, right?'

'Not definitively.'

Paul stops shaving. 'It's just that now I'm not going to be here, I'm worried . . . What if they don't let you stay here? Do you know what I mean? You can't stay like this for ever.'

'No, it's not for ever,' I tell him.

'But it could be for ever.'

'I wouldn't accept it for ever like this,' I say.

'But you've accepted it for twelve years now. So don't you think that maybe this is the time you could leave?'

'Yes, eventually.'

Paul starts shaving again.

'You know, I've found a place for you to live in Paris. I went to it the other day. It's in the centre of Paris. It's an apartment complex and there are a lot of other people who had immigration problems, like

235

you; refugees, and they live there. The rooms are not very big, but they're lockable, and there's a bed and space for books, and closets for all your things. And I talked to them about you. They said that if you wanted to go there, they'd help you. You'd have a place and we could arrange food, and someone could come and clean the place.'

'I cannot get in,' I tell him. 'I cannot get into France.'

'But Alfred, this is the thing – I think you can.'

'By the judgement, I cannot. I'm sort of expelled from France.'

'Alfred, there is a bed for you at this place.'

I take cream from tube and rub it onto my chin. 'There are beds everywhere.'

'I know, but not in the airport.'

'In the airport there's Hotel Cocoon,' I tell him.

'But you're not in the hotel. You're on the bench.'

'Yes, because it's cheaper.'

I bend down to the sink and wash my face.

'But the thing I'm trying to say is that I can arrange for the people at this place to take you in.'

'You cannot arrange anything,' I say.

'Alfred, you know that I care about you, don't you? You know I care what happens to you?' says Paul. 'We've spent a lot of time together. I didn't just come in here and leave after we spoke for a week or two. We've spent six months together making this film. I care about you, and being stuck on a bench at an airport is not a life for you.'

'You'd better talk about Britain,' I tell him. 'How can I go back to Britain?'

'Alfred, do you want to leave the airport or not?'

236

I rub my face. 'My destination is not clear yet. Where I'll go from here.'

'That's the thing; I don't want to leave the airport without you knowing what you're going to do. I can help you. The people running this place in Paris, they said they can handle it – they're experts in this sort of thing. You could sleep there.'

I check my hair and my moustache.

'I've finished, excuse me. See you later.' I want to leave the washroom now.

'Wait for me a second. Does it upset you that I say these things? I don't mean to upset you.'

'No.'

'I don't know what to do, Alfred.'

'Individually, I cannot do anything. I have big challenge by France. That organization you're talking about – what can they do? France refused me before; they'll refuse again.'

I notice a hair on my jumper and brush it off with my hand.

'But the thing is, I spoke to these people, Alfred. I asked them myself.'

I tell him, 'I don't care about people.'

I lean forward and spit into the sink. Paul is quiet now.

'You talked about me being accepted by England before, now you change. You talked about me being accepted by France, something about Belgium, something about Germany. I'm not wandering. I don't wander.'

I don't want to be in washroom any more so I say, 'See you later.'

I walk away from Paul, past Glen who is holding

the second camera, and down a corridor. Then I come back, smile at Glen and say, 'How was it? Do you think you got the scene?'

Glen nods.

4th July 2003

I am sitting in the middle of Charles de Gaulle airport using a biro pen to cut open my head.

The lump on my head is very big now and it is painful if I touch it or lie on it. Sometimes this makes it difficult to sleep. It is full of a bad infection.

It is late in the evening and there are few people left in the terminal, so no-one will pass by and see. I bought a biro pen today, and a small bottle of anti-septic, and some cotton wool from the pharmacy.

Dr Bargain has offered to treat the infection, but I do not want to go to the medical centre. It is better if I can treat it myself.

I take the pen in one hand and I hold the small mirror that I use when trimming my hair in the other. If I am careful, then I can just about see what I am doing. I press the point of the pen down onto the lump; it feels hard and solid and hurts when I touch it. I press down and the skin strains. I press harder and the pen goes through the skin. The infection bursts out. It smells bad.

I squeeze the base and edges of the lump. More in-fection comes out and I wipe it away with some clean tissue. When the lump is gone, I put some antiseptic on a piece of cotton wool and apply it to the cut. It stings. I mop up the blood with tissues and put them in an old McDonald's bag that I have kept for this purpose.

The next morning Glen comes to see me. I have not

seen him for a long time. I take the tissues out of the bag and show him the infection. Paul's father is a doctor; he has offered many times to ask his father to come and look at the problem, but now there is no need because I have lanced the lump with a biro pen.

Glen has brought me some clothes, fresh and washed from the cleaners, and says that the film we made gained a special nomination for the Michael Powell Award for Best New Director at the 2001 Edinburgh Film Festival, which is a good success.

He says, 'How are you?'

I say, 'Fine.'

He asks me what I have been doing.

I say, 'Waiting for my documentation. What else can I do?'

Before he goes Glen gives me photocopy of an article about the film that we made together. This is because he knows that I like to receive articles about my situation so that I can keep them in my files in my boxes.

At the end of the article there is a quote from a photographer called Manoocher Deghati. He says: 'Alfred's story symbolizes the story of millions of Iranians who have left their country for different reasons and have sought asylum abroad. Although his is of course an extreme case. While he's been here I've talked to many people, Iranians and other friends who have wanted to help him. But they all say that he rejects their help. He believes he has given himself up to the hands of destiny and wants to continue this kind of life. Now after eleven years he's really lost.'

I do not know why he says I am lost. I know where I am. I am in Terminal One, Charles de Gaulle airport. Simple.

Diary extract

'9:05 a.m. I hear on the news on my radio that part of Terminal 2E, Charles de Gaulle airport has collapsed and five people have been killed. Radio said, "A section of roof collapsed sending slabs of concrete and metal crashing down to the floor of a departure lounge. The terminal was hailed as a technological wonder when it first opened eleven months ago."

Terminal 2E is very close, only 2km away from Terminal One. I would like to go and observe what has occurred, but I cannot leave my possessions unattended because I am not in a secure place. Over many years in airport I have accumulated much baggage. Boxes of newspapers and magazines. Boxes of my diaries. Bags of books. My collection of soda tops. I cannot leave them in unsecure area so I cannot go to Terminal 2E.'

Chapter 22

22nd February 2004

I am sitting on my red bench from the Bye Bye Bar in the middle of Charles de Gaulle airport, reading page 96 of the French language version of a biography of the Empress Farah, the wife of the Shah of Iran. I am using my French/English dictionary to assist my translation and improve my French.

It is a Sunday afternoon and the shops on the boutique level are closed. It is the quietest that the airport ever gets. I look up and see Matthew Rose walking towards me.

Matthew Rose is a writer and also an artist. He has written articles about my situation before. One was in the *New York Times* magazine. Once he gave me a book about Thomas Jefferson, the third President of America. Another time he gave me a collage he had made which showed the Queen of England sitting on a chair with a human intestine coming out of her foot.

'Hello, Alfred. How are you? Do you have a moment?'

People who visit me cannot make an appointment, but I have been sitting here for fifteen years; when they have found me once, then they know where to find me again.

Matthew sits hunched over my little black table that was given to me by special dispensation when they closed down the Bye Bye Bar. On my table is a plastic drinking cup, and standing inside the cup are: three McDonald's drinking straws in their paper wrappers, four sachets of sugar, three sachets of salt, two sachets of pepper, one sachet of ketchup, and three sets of a plastic knife, fork, spoon and white paper napkin, each sealed in a plastic wrapper.

Matthew has sheets of A4-sized white paper with a question handwritten in red ink at the top of each page. It is the same size paper as Dr Bargain used to give me to write my journal on, before he stopped

giving it to me and I got paper from a man at Thai
Airlines instead, who also gave me a pen.

'Alfred?'

'Yes.'

'These questions are from the New York editor of
Premiere magazine. Have you seen *Premiere* magazine?'

'No.'

'Well, that doesn't matter; it's a big film publication
that tells people all about new movies. Now, I know
we've covered some of these before, but these are
questions from my editor. Is that all right with you?
Are you excited about the film?'

'Yes. Of course. It will be good for my image.'

'And has having the money from the film deal
changed your life here at the airport?'

I look around. It is quiet, but every few minutes
people wander by. I do not know who they are.

'I can buy anything that I want now, but I have a
security problem here. It's not a safe area, because
things can be lost or stolen.'

'Have you had anything stolen?'

'Yes. It was very bad. I had one bag stolen.'

'A whole suitcase?'

'No, a plastic bag.'

'What was in it?'

'*Time* magazine.'

'Just a *Time* magazine?'

'Three different copies.'

'Has anything else been stolen?'

'My pipe.'

'You lost another pipe?'

'No, just one. I lost it three years ago.'

Matthew makes some notes on his paper.

'Did Steven Spielberg ever come over to Paris to meet you?'

'No. I haven't seen him.'

'What's your favourite Spielberg film?'

'I have not seen a Spielberg film.'

Matthew pulls a face. 'Never? Not even before you were here? What about *Jaws*? Or *E.T.*? *E.T.* is extraterrestrial; it's about a strange being that came and got lost on Earth, and these children found him and became friends with him. Do you know that one?'

'I didn't watch it.'

Matthew makes notes on his paper.

'In a newspaper I read an article on *A.I.* Spielberg film about a lost robot boy who wants to be accepted as real and find his true origin,' I say.

'Did you like the sound of that film?' asks Matthew. I say, 'Yes.'

'OK, Alfred, did Tom Hanks come over to talk to you for research?'

'No.'

'Have you ever seen any famous people at the airport?'

'Sure. Probably many famous people.'

'Like?'

'Like Tom Hanks.'

'You saw Tom Hanks?'

'Yes.'

'Where?'

'On a bus. He was on a bus going to another terminal. His face was at the window.'

'Wow. Tom Hanks was right here in Paris but he didn't say hello to you, even though he's kind of playing a version of you? Tom Hanks came all the way

244

over from America, but he didn't even stop to say hello or ask you any questions?' Matthew scribbles very quickly. 'Anyone else? Any other famous people?'

I say, 'Catherine Zeta-Jones.'

'Catherine Zeta-Jones? Here? At the airport?'

'Yes.'

Matthew scribbles more excited notes.

'Where did you see her?'

I point to the newsagent's and the big red sign that says RELAY. 'She was buying a newspaper? Just over there?'

Matthew scribbles more notes, his hand racing across the page and back, across the page and back. Then he looks at what he has written. He looks over at the small newsagent's, and at the display case full of models of the Eiffel Tower produced from blue plastic.

'Are you sure it was her?'

'Yes.'

He thinks for a few seconds longer and then he says, 'Was it Catherine Zeta-Jones, or maybe a woman who looked like her?'

'It was her.'

'Or maybe it was a woman who just looked like her? I know a lot of people look like other people?'

I shrug. 'Yes,' I say. 'Possibly a woman that looks like another woman.'

Matthew thinks for a moment.

'Alfred, do you know what Catherine Zeta-Jones looks like?'

'No.'

He crosses out half a page of notes and then looks at the top half of the page.

'Do you know what Tom Hanks looks like?'

'No.'

He crosses out what he has written on the top half of the page and takes a deep breath.

16th September 1952

I am standing on the bow of a boat sailing out into the Strait of Hormoz at the southern end of the Persian Gulf. I am eight years old and the sun is shining on my face.

Behind us is the port of Bandar, where my father gave money to a fisherman to take us on his boat. We had missed the lunchtime ferry and are now at sea in a boat that smells of dead fish. I do not like the smell and I do not like the fact that the deck of the boat is slippery with fish scales. Ahead of us across the blue water is Hormoz Island, getting bigger and bigger. This is the first time I have been here.

I look through the rippling heat haze and I see an oil tanker slowly creeping into view, becoming larger and larger on the horizon like a building that is sailing through the water. At least, I think I remember the oil tanker. I am not sure when I saw the oil tanker; maybe it was a different crossing. When I think of the memory again, there is no tanker.

As the boat cuts through the water, my father sits down next to me, takes out his pipe and begins to tell me a story.

'The fortress on Hormoz Island was built by a man called Afonso the Great, who was the admiral of a great sea fleet. He lived a long, long time ago. In the year 1507, he came and laid siege to the island of Hormoz because he wanted to conquer it for the Portuguese. Do you know what a siege is?'

'Yes, it's when people surround somewhere and won't let someone out.'

'Afonso the Great won the battle and began building a mighty fortress on the island, a castle so big and so strong that it took eight years just to build it. It was finally finished in the year 1515, and for more than one hundred years this castle meant that the Portuguese could control the international trading routes – the way that people sold things to each other – through the entire Gulf of Persia. Many people became rich. When the castle had stood there for fifty years, a mighty army from Ottoman Empire besieged the fortress for one entire month.'

'Did they get inside?'

'No, the castle was too strong. It has now been standing for five hundred years. I remember my father bringing me here when I was your age, and now I am bringing you.'

The fishing boat ties up to the jetty and my father helps me jump from the boat to the land. We walk around the edge of the waterfront where there are many fishing boats tied up. Bits of fish that have been pecked clean by seabirds lie on the decks of the empty boats.

We follow the curve of the waterfront until it becomes just a rocky ledge, and we walk along it over the sea. We come to a large open-air courtyard with a building on the left-hand side.

'That was the armoury where they kept all the weapons,' says my father.

There is a path marked by stones and I run along it, racing ahead of my father. I want to see where it leads.

25th July 2004

I am sitting on my red bench from the Bye Bye Bar in the middle of Charles de Gaulle airport, waiting to see what will happen.

I am waiting for a green card so I can go to America. I am waiting for a British passport so I can go to England. I am waiting for my documentation so I can go anywhere.

I have been sitting on my red bench from the Bye Bye Bar, in the middle of Charles de Gaulle airport waiting to leave for nearly sixteen years.

I am reading a letter from my bag. It is a letter that I received six years ago.

This is what the letter says:

Thursday 25th July 1998

Dear Alfred,

I read the article about your plight and long time existence in Charles de Gaulle Airport. No doubt you will have had other responses besides mine and it is possible that your mother may have read it also.

Alfred life is so short and it is quite obvious you have endured a great deal. Please don't give up now. Trust your solicitor (legal advisor and the chaplain) and believe in yourself. Let them take you to Brussels to get your Titre des Voyage and permit. Then come to Britain and find your mother. Do you imagine for one moment she has forgotten you! She must herself have been a courageous young nurse to be working at that time in Iran. To have left you behind must have been devastating for her. You may have half-

248

brothers and half-sisters somewhere.

In my heart I hope she comes to find you to re-generate that willpower within you to look forward not back.

Only you can help yourself now, don't despair, you had a goal, follow your dream and step out-side of this insularity. You deserve better.

Be positive now Alfred, I so want your story to have a happy ending. Can't you feel my hands patting you gently and urging you warmly not to look a gift horse in the mouth.

With sincere good wishes for your happiness.

Carol Richards
Potters Bar
Herts,
UK

I remember being in a library in Brussels many years ago and meeting a man. I cannot remember any-thing about the man I spoke to except that he was wearing a dark suit and his shoulders were wide, but his head was narrow like a pencil. I still do not think this can be correct. Since that meeting I have tried to discover information and the point of origin of Miss Semon.

I wrote several letters. This is the reply I received from British authorities:

General Register Office
St Catherine's House
10 Kingsway
London
WC2B 6JP

Your reference: CAS
Date: 22 Nov 1984

Dear Sir/Madam
I refer to your application of 16.11.1984 in which you ask for the birth certificate of Miss Semon. It will help us in our search for the appropriate entry if you will kindly provide the particulars requested overleaf and return this form to us.
　Yours faithfully
　F. Bromley

I did not know the particulars that they requested overleaf. I did not even know if Miss Semon is the correct spelling, or if Miss Semone is the correct spelling. Or even if it should be 'Simon'.

I would like to find the woman who is really my mother before it is too late. I am nearly sixty. The woman who is really my mother must be eighty-three years old. I think that when a person gets older, sometimes they think more of the past.

16th September 1952
I run along the path ahead of my father and I am suddenly on the ramparts of the fortress. All around the edge are cannon emplacements. The guns face into the ocean so that they could target any approaching ships. This is where soldiers stood five centuries ago, keeping vigil day and night, watching the ocean for the approach of enemy ships.

I can see a dozen tiny ships dotted around in the dark blue waters of the Gulf; mostly fishing boats pursued by swarms of hungry birds. Looking north I can see Bandar on the edge of the mainland, a thin patchwork of boats and houses hugging the coastline. Looking south is a view over the village of Hormoz; tiny flat-roofed houses dazzle in the sunlight. Behind the village, the mountains in the centre of the island suddenly burst into the blue sky, looking sharp and broken.

I was going to hide from my father and play a game, but now I am too busy looking. I can see the whole world from here.

My father sees an old man coming up the stairway and goes over to him. I see my father put some money, a few coins, into his hand, and then my father beckons to me to follow them. We go back down the stone stairs and stop by a door by a sign that says Water Supply. I am thirsty, but I do not want to see a water supply. The old man looks at me and smiles as he reaches into his pocket and feels around to pull out a heavy bunch of keys. He unlocks the door and pushes it open. He gestures for us to enter.

'*Befamayid.*'

Inside it is cool, very cool. I walk down a spiral stone staircase, going slowly so that my eyes can get used to the dark. It twists and turns round and round like the inside of a long seashell. We go down and down and down.

At the bottom of the staircase, I step out and find myself leaning against a wooden barrier. The old man takes a torch from a holder on the wall and lights it. The flames burst into life.

Now I can see the most extraordinary thing. We are in a huge cavern. It seems to me as a child that it is vast. Perhaps it is the size of a football pitch across.

Around the roughly circular edge is a raised platform that you can walk on. I can hear the sound of dripping water falling regularly like a tick of a clock. The air smells cool, but somehow very clean, like in a garden. There are pillars of rock that support the roof. We stay inside for a long time. I cannot tell how much time has gone by in this dark place under the ground.

On the way back to Bandar we catch the regular ferry. The sun is still bright, but it is cooler now. I stand at the aft of the ferry and watch the island getting smaller and smaller.

My father leans down and whispers into my ear, 'When you have not seen the sea for a long time, then think of this moment.'

25th July 2004

When it is hot inside Terminal One, Charles de Gaulle airport, I think of the cave that was cool. When it is cold inside Terminal One, Charles de Gaulle airport, I think of standing on the ship, and the sun on my face that was warm.

Perhaps you are reading this book on a train? Perhaps you are sitting in a park? Perhaps you are in a library? I do not know where you are reading it. But wherever you are, you can know that right now, at this very moment, as your eyes are reading these words across the page – as you read this word, that word, this word – you can know that I am here sitting on my red bench from the Bye Bye Bar, in the middle of Charles de Gaulle airport, waiting to leave.

Passengers are reminded to keep their personal baggage with them at all times.

At lunchtime today I had a Filet-o-fish. I had this

because it is better than the chicken. I also had an order of French fries. I put a sachet of salt into the plastic drinking cup on my table, so that now inside the cup are: two McDonald's drinking straws in their paper wrappers, three sachets of sugar, two sachets of salt, two sachets of pepper, one sachet of ketchup, and three sets of a plastic knife, fork, spoon and napkin, each sealed in a clear plastic wrapper. My collection of straws and soda tops are hidden behind my bench where they are safe.

Dr Bargain said to me once, 'Alfred, is it not strange that after all the newspaper articles, after all the television and radio interviews, that not one person in sixteen years has come forward to say, "Ah, that Sir Alfred! I know him." No-one has ever tried to get in touch with you from your past. No family. No friend. No doctor. Nothing. Alfred, it is like you suddenly materialized from nowhere to sit here in the airport.'

Perhaps someone reading this book will know something about the woman who is really my mother and write to the publishers of the book. Perhaps the man I wrote this book with will come to the airport one day and give me a letter detailing my point of origin. Perhaps he will not. I do not know.

8th August 1988
7:40 p.m. It is evening and the airport is getting quieter. Planes are leaving, but no new passengers are arriving. The man in the Burger King clears the wrappers and rubbish that customers have left on the tables and then wipes the tables with a damp cloth. I am the only customer left.

I walk to the counter of Burger King. The staff are in

253

the back cleaning the machines and cooking devices. When one of them sees me waiting, he shakes his head.

The terminal is shaped like a large ring and I walk right around the basement level in a circuit to see what is down there, and then I come back up the stairs.

Outside, the sky is getting dark. Just near Burger King are the long benches where I was sitting this morning, waiting for my plane to England. I go over and sit down. I put my shoulder bag with some clothes in it at one end, and then lie on my side along the bench, using my bag as a pillow.

It is not a usual proposition to sleep in an airport, but it is only for one night.